MIX
Papier aus verantwortungsvollen Quellen
Paper from responsible sources
FSC® C105338

Diana Eunice Kawenda

Legal reception and regional economic integration in Southern Africa

Anchor Academic
Publishing

Kawenda, Diana Eunice: Legal reception and regional economic integration in Southern Africa, Hamburg, Anchor Academic Publishing 2017

Buch-ISBN: 978-3-96067-158-9
PDF-eBook-ISBN: 978-3-96067-658-4
Druck/Herstellung: Anchor Academic Publishing, Hamburg, 2017

Bibliografische Information der Deutschen Nationalbibliothek:
Die Deutsche Nationalbibliothek verzeichnet diese Publikation in der Deutschen Nationalbibliografie; detaillierte bibliografische Daten sind im Internet über http://dnb.d-nb.de abrufbar.

Bibliographical Information of the German National Library:
The German National Library lists this publication in the German National Bibliography. Detailed bibliographic data can be found at: http://dnb.d-nb.de

Hermannstal 119k, 22119 Hamburg
http://www.diplomica-verlag.de, Hamburg 2017
Printed in Germany

DEDICATION

To my one and only daughter Makunda and my nephew Lolo, both of whom passed away at the height of this research on the 25th of April 2015 in a car accident. I have used my loss as a stepping stone to greater things.

ACKNOWLEDGMENTS

Firstly, I would like to thank my creator for being my guide and shield throughout my studies. Much appreciation goes to the staff and the great intellectual minds at the NWU (faculty of law) Potchefstroom Campus for their unwavering support, courtesy and concern over my work. At the heart of this study lies the expertise of Dr HJ Lubbe, who took time and exercised his patience with me, in moulding my research capabilities over the past two years. I am sincerely grateful for the effort you put in. Secondly, to Dr M Barnard, you came through for me at a time when I felt stuck and you guided me in how I ought to lay out my ideas. You have been supportive of my personal growth and have motivated me to pursue my academic career. I also extend my gratitude to Prof Stephen De la Harpe, who always encouraged me to keep going, even when I felt like giving up.

To George and Lucy Kawenda, my parents - I thank you for always being there for me. Thank you for the financial, moral and spiritual support. I owe much to you guys.

To Fungai Mahiya, Getrude Shoko, Takudzwa Taruza, Majory Dzingai, Tirivenyu Mutema, Caiphas Soyapi with whom I walked this journey thank you for hearing me out and giving me assistance when needed.

ABSTRACT

The dire African economic situation has been a perennial problem for the past six decades. Many problems emanate from slow economic growth, such as poverty and unemployment. There is a need for a collective effort to ensure economic growth, which would be the most viable solution to these problems, and the key to such a collective effort is regional economic integration (REI). This study examines REI within the legal context. It tests the proposition that the law can be used as a means to achieving REI. At the heart of this proposition lies the legal challenge that comes with the different approaches to legal reception and how they impede the realisation of REI. An analysis is performed of the theories related to legal reception, which include the monist, the dualist and the hybrid theories. REI was embraced in Europe and has yielded fruitful results. There is no doubt that the collective efforts to realise economic growth in other continents stems from the inspiration of the European example. Europe is used in this study to illustrate how the obstacles that accompany the different approaches to legal reception may be superseded. The study examines how the law was used in Europe as a means to attain REI. An attempt is then made to understand REI from an African perspective by setting out the legal framework and its shortcomings. Attention is paid to Africa's sub-region of Southern Africa, and the study examines legal reception within Southern Africa and how the different approaches to legal reception within the two RECs, the SADC and COMESA, impact upon the realisation of REI. It seeks to evaluate the possibility that the African continent, particularly Southern Africa, may be able to use the law to attain REI. A further analysis is made by examining South Africa's approach to legal reception and how this impacts on the realisation of REI.

Key words: REI, legal integration, legal reception, monism, dualism, SADC, COMESA

OPSOMMING

Die nypende ekonomiese situasie in Afrika het vir die afgelope ses dekades reeds 'n ewigdurende probleem geword. Talle probleme soos armoede en werkloosheid ontstaan weens stadige ekonomiese groei. 'n Kollektiewe poging is noodsaaklik om ekonomiese groei, wat die lewensvatbaarste oplossing vir hierdie probleem sou wees, te verseker, en ook die sleutel tot so 'n kollektiewe poging is streeksekonomiese integrasie (SEI) (regional economic integration – REI). Hierdie studie ondersoek SEI binne die regskonteks. Dit toets die proposisie dat die reg aangewend kan word as 'n wyse om SEI te bewerkstellig. Aan die kern van hierdie proposisie lê die regsuitdaging wat gepaard gaan met die verskillende benaderings tot regsaanvaarding en hoedat dit die bewerkstelliging van SEI kniehalter. 'n Analise van die teorieë wat met regsaanvaarding verband hou, is uitgevoer, wat die monis-, die dualis- en die hibried-teorie insluit. SEI is in Europa aanvaar en het vrugbare resultate opgelewer. Daar bestaan geen twyfel daaroor dat die kollektiewe pogings om ekonomiese groei in ander kontinente uit die inspirasie van die Europese voorbeeld voortspruit nie. Europa is in hierdie studie as voorbeeld geneem om te illustreer hoedat die struikelblokke wat met die verskillende benaderings tot regsaanvaarding gepaard gaan, uit die weg geruim kan word. Die studie ondersoek hoedat die reg in Europa benut is as 'n metode om SEI te bewerkstellig. 'n Poging is toe aangewend om SEI vanuit 'n Afrika-perspektief te verstaan deur die regsraamwerk en die tekortkominge daarvan uiteen te sit. Aandag is geskenk aan Afrika se substreek, Suidelike Afrika, en die studie ondersoek regsaanvaarding binne Suidelike Afrika en hoe die verskillende benaderings tot regsaanvaarding binne die twee RECs, SADC en COMESA, 'n impak het op die totstandkoming van SEI. Dit poog om die moontlikheid te ondersoek dat die Afrika-kontinent, in besonder Suidelike Afrika, die reg kan benut om SEI te bewerkstellig. 'n Verdere analise is gedoen deur Suid-Afrika se benadering tot regsaanvaarding te ondersoek en hoedat dit 'n impak het op die totstandkoming van SEI.

Sleutelwoorde: SEI, regsintegrasie, regsaanvaarding, monisme, dualisme, SADC, COMESA

TABLE OF CONTENTS

LIST OF FIGURES

LIST OF TABLES

LIST OF ABBREVIATIONS

ACHR	African Charter on Human Rights
AFDB	African Development Bank
AI	African Insight
Am'J'Int 'L	American Journal of International Law
AU	African Union
BIT	Bilateral Investment Treaties
CEN-SAD	Community of Sahel–Saharan States
CILSA	Comparative International Law in Southern Africa
COMESA	Common Market for Eastern and Southern Africa
Duke J I L	Duke Journal of International Law
EAC	East African Community
ECA	Economic Commission on Africa
ECCAS	Economic Community of Central African States
ECJ	European Court of Justice
ECOSOC	Economic and Social Council of the United Nations
ECSC	European Coal and Steel Community
EEC	European Economic Community
EJEL	European Journal of Economic Law
EJIL	European Journal of International Law

EU	European Union
Fordham Int L J	Fordham International Law Journal
FTA	Free Trade Area
GATT	General Agreement on Tariffs and Trade
ICSS	International Commission on International State Sovereignty
IGAD	Intergovernmental Authority on Development
IO	International Organisation
J Comp .L	Journal on Comparative Law
JEPP	Journal of European Public Policy
J'Int L &Com	Journal of International Law and Commerce
LDD	Law Democracy and Development
Mizan L Rev	Mizan Law Review
MTSP	Medium Term Strategic Plan
NGHC	North Gauteng High Court
NPT	Treaty on the Non-Proliferation of Nuclear Weapons
PELJ	Potchefstroom Electronic Law Journal
PER	Potchefstroom Elektroniese Regsblad
POCCA	Proceeds of Criminal Civil Confiscation Act
REC	Regional Economic Community
RECs	Regional Economic Communities
REI	Regional Economic Integration

RISDP	Regional Indicative Strategic Development Plan
SACU	Southern African Customs Union
SADC	Southern African Development Community
SAGJ	South African Geographical Journal
SAPL	South African Public Law
SARS	South Africa Revenue Services
SAYIL	South African Yearbook of International Law
SCA	Supreme Court of Appeal
Syr J of Int L and Com	Syracuse Journal of International Law and Commerce
UGBC	Universitatis George Bacovia Juridica
U.III L.F	University of Illinois Law Forum
UMA	Arab Maghreb Union
Va J Int'l L	Virginia Journal of International Law
VCLT	Vienna Convention on the Law of Treaties
WTO	World Trade Organisation
ZaoRV	Heidelberg Journal of International Law

Chapter 1: Introduction

The endless cycle of poverty and slow economic growth has been a perennial feature of the African continent ever since the post-colonial period.[1] Marking the inception of the decolonisation process of Africa in early 1960's, Africa was and still remains a continent that is fragmented as a result of the colonial powers dividing the continent, forming new states which had small populations and small incomes resulting from their narrow markets.[2]

The fragmentation of the continent proved to be the main stumbling block to economic growth and poverty alleviation in the continent. From 1970-1979 Sub-Saharan Africa's GDP per capita declined to 0.7%.[3]From 1980 to 1989 the economic situation worsened, with the economic growth rate falling to -1.0%.[4]

The economic situation of the African continent was a cause for concern not only for the Pan African leaders,[5] but also for the international community at large. The United Nations (UN) set up the United Nations Economic Commission on Africa (UNECA), whose primary objective was to come up with probable solutions to Africa's dire economic situation of economic decline.

The UNECA considered the major impediment to Africa's development to be the narrowed markets of most states, which made it impossible for some states to grow economically and recommended that the continent embrace Regional Economic Integration (REI) as a strategy that would lead to economic growth and the subsequent eradication of poverty within the continent.[6] REI is a collective effort made by different states that fall within the same geographical location to co-ordinate their economic activities as a means to ensure the development of the regions and states involved.[7]

---

1 Bauer *Is there a vicious circle of poverty?* 4.
2 Hatzernburg 2011 http://www.wto.org.
3 Kritzinger and Van Niekerk World Bank Country Report.
4 Kritzinger and Van Niekerk World Bank Country Report.
5 The founding fathers of the OAU: President Nkurumah, Emperor Haile Selassie, Fulbert Youlou, Julius Nyerere, and many more.
6 http://www.uneca.org.
7 See detailed discussion in para 2.2 of this study.

The notion of REI was well received by the Organisation of African Unity (OAU)[8] heads of states, although the Organisation's primary objective was to ensure political co-operation aimed at maintaining post-colonial independence by seeing to it that the colonial period would never re-emerge in the continent.

The efforts made by the OAU to pursue REI are evidenced in the signing of the Lagos Plan of Action, which detailed the manner in which REI was to be pursued in the continent.[9] REI was acknowledged to be achievable at sub-regional level, a decision which saw the proliferation of Regional Economic Communities (RECs) in Africa, all of which had the main goal of ensuring economic growth and development for their people through REI.[10]

Although the idea of REI has been favourably considered and steps have been taken to pilot the process of achieving it, the underlying problems which REI seeks to solve still exist. There is a strange anomaly in Africa to the effect that there have been accelerated economic growth rates (in 2013 the average African growth rate was double the global average),[11] but at the heart of this fast growing economy is a large population still living in poverty.[12] Perhaps there is a relation between this situation and the fact that four decades have passed since REI was acknowledged as a strategy that would address Africa's economic problems, and yet REI has not been fully established at either sub-regional level or continental level.

Currently the endless cycle of poverty still permeates Southern Africa. The recently published Sustainable Development Goals (SDG) for 2016-2030 still lists poverty eradication at the top of Southern Africa's main goals.[13] REI initiatives in Southern Africa have been made, as evidenced by the two RECs that have been formally recognised by

---

8 The OAU was succeeded by the African Union (AU) upon the signing of the *Constitutive Act*.

9 Hartzenberg 2011 http://www.wto.org. "The ambition of African leaders to integrate Africa and to develop the continent through import substitution and industrialisation was a key feature of the immediate post-colonial period and provided the rationale for the Lagos Plan of Action."

10 World Bank African Regional Report on the Sustainable Development Goals.

11 McKinsey &Company "Africa's growth acceleration was widespread, with 27 of its 30 largest economies expanding more rapidly after 2000.

12 World Bank African Regional Report on the Sustainable Development Goals.

13 World Bank African Regional Report on the Sustainable Development Goals.

the African Union (AU),[14] namely the Southern African Development Community (SADC)[15] and the Common Market for Eastern and Southern Africa (COMESA).[16]

Despite having institutions set up to steer the REI agenda forward, one realises that the main problems which these institutions are designed to overcome are still prevalent, as evidenced by the continuing need to eradicate poverty in Africa in the Southern African region. Of late, political and economic solutions have been proposed, but not much emphasis has been placed on the legal problems that are making the attainment of REI a challenge.

The main legal hurdle has to do with the fact the laws that govern REI are not uniformly applied and therefore lack certainty. This limits the effectiveness of REI. The lack of certainty emanates from the fact that member states have different legal cultures that prescribe different approaches on how international treaties will have force and effect within member states' municipal laws. There are two main theories that determine legal reception - the monist and the dualist theory - but some states follow a hybrid approach where they simultaneously apply both theories.

This study seeks to determine how the different approaches to legal reception prescribed by the two Southern African RECs impact upon the realisation of REI. The study also evaluates the proposition that if REI laws were to be uniformly applied (legal integration), and then REI would be attainable. Legal integration is wholly dependent on legal reception in that legal integration will be achievable when the process of receiving Regional Economic Community (REC)laws ensures uniformity and consistency. Perhaps this would be one means of realising the SDG post 2015, and it might lead to the attainment of a deeper form of REI that would be effective in changing the economic

---

14 Department of International Relations 2003 http://www.dfa.gov.za The RECs include: Community of Sahel-Saharan States (CEN-SAD), Economic Community of Central African States (ECCAS), Common Market for Eastern and Southern Africa (COMESA), Economic Community of West African States (ECOWAS), Intergovernmental Authority for Development(IGAD), Southern African Development Community (SADC) and the Union du Maghreb Arab (UMA).

15 SADC 2012 http://www.sadc.int.The member states are Angola, Botswana, Democratic Republic of Congo, Lesotho, Madagascar, Malawi, Mauritius, Mozambique, Namibia, Seychelles, South Africa, Swaziland, United Republic of Tanzania, Zambia and Zimbabwe.

16 COMESA http://about.comesa.int. The member states are Burundi, Comoros, Democratic Republic of Congo, Djibouti, Egypt, Eritrea, Ethiopia, Kenya, Libya, Madagascar, Rwanda, Seychelles, Sudan, Swaziland, Uganda, Zambia, and Zimbabwe.

status of the African continent and ultimately resolving the problem of slow economic growth and the high levels of poverty which currently mar Southern Africa.

To determine if the law can be used as a strategy to implement REI for the attainment of the SDG post 2015, chapter 2 of this study will serve as an introductory chapter to the phenomenon of REI by defining what REI entails. There is a need to determine the relation between REI and the law. Can REI be viewed through a legal prism? As REI involves interstate relations, the legal theories and concepts that relate to international law will be central to this chapter. The concept of legal reception will be defined, bearing in mind that the member states of RECs have their own way of receiving international law into their own municipal legal systems, which implies that there is a need to rehearse the legal theories that relate to legal reception, which are the monist theory, the dualist theory and the hybrid theory, by setting out their differences and how each of them impacts upon REI.

It is an undeniable fact that the longest-standing example of a successful REC is the European Economic Community (EEC), from which all other emerging RECs draw inspiration. Chapter 2 will analyse the principles of REI within the European context. At the inception of the European Economic Community (EEC) there were divergent approaches to legal reception, a fact which posed a legal hurdle to the attainment of uniformity in the REI laws. Despite this challenge, the EEC was able to attain legal integration as a means to REI. Was legal integration a plausible solution? If so, how was it achieved within the EEC context? This analysis will later serve as a template for the Southern Africa's RECs, which are faced by the strikingly similar legal challenges that arise as a result of their different approaches to legal reception.

It is of importance to note that a wholly Eurocentric approach to REI is impossible, as REIs tend to be tempered by historical and political differences. The Europe of today could not fruitfully be compared with the Africa of today. It took decades before Europe ultimately formed a Union, thus marking the completion of the REI process. This is the main reason why this study focuses on the EEC, which was the predecessor of the EU, to determine how legal reception in the early stages of REI formation in Europe was dealt with.

Furthermore, the legal cultures of the member states of the Southern African RECs are direct descendants of those of the European states which were their former colonisers, ultimately resulting in their having the same approach to legal reception.

The second part of this study, Chapter 3, will analyse REI within the African context and how it has been applied from a continental point of view. Narrowing the scope of this study, the focus will be placed on the two RECs recognised by the AU in Southern Africa, namely the SADC and the COMESA.[17] There is also the Southern African Customs Union (SACU), which is another REC within Southern Africa, but for the purpose of this dissertation the SACU will not be referred to because it is the smallest REC in Southern Africa[18] and all the member states of the SACU belong to either the SADC or COMESA.[19]

Chapter 3 will also analyse the overall approach to legal reception in Southern Africa and make a determination of which approach is predominantly used within the sub region and how it impacts on REI by constantly referring to the EEC example set out in Chapter 2. The chapter will also evaluate legal reception in the SADC and COMESA with reference to landmark rulings in this regard.

Chapter 4, which is the last part of this study, will focus chiefly on one of the member states within Southern Africa, will determine how at municipal level it adopts legal reception of international law, and will determine how its approach to legal reception leads to the attainment of REI. The country of focus will be South Africa, which has been considered as the unchallenged "economic heavyweight of the region".[20] Most exports and imports within the region either come from or go to South Africa, thus showing that the completion of the REI process in Southern Africa would stand to South Africa's economic benefit.

---

17 Department of International Relations 2003 http://www.dfa.gov.za The RECs are: Community of Sahel-Saharan States(CEN-SAD), Economic Community of Central African States(ECCAS), Common Market for Eastern and Southern Africa(COMESA), Economic Community of West African States(ECOWAS), Intergovernmental Authority for Development(IGAD), Southern African Development Community(SADC) and the Union du Maghreb Arab(UMA).

18 Department of International Relations 2003 http://www.dfa.gov.za.

19 Department of International Relations 2003 http://www.dfa.gov.za.

20 Current status of key economic Indicators-Regional Economic Trends 2014.

To evaluate South Africa's approach to legal reception, reference will be made to South Africa's constitutional framework. Can South Africa's approach to legal reception lead to the realisation of REI? Cases from the Supreme Court of Appeal (SCA) and the Constitutional Court (CC) will be discussed. Does South Africa value the need to uphold its regional obligations so as to ultimately realise REI and achieve the SDG post 2015? Chapter 4 may contribute to the constitutional development of South Africa as it is an in-depth evaluation of South Africa's constitutional provisions and how they can be used to further REI in Southern Africa.

This research will be carried out by means of a comparative study between the EEC and the Southern African REI process. As mentioned earlier on, the main reason for comparing the EEC with the RECs in Southern Africa is because REI in the EEC was a success, and numerous subsequent RECs have been inspired by the European example. A comparison will be drawn between the legal aspects of REI in Southern Africa and those of the EEC. The main reason for comparing the two areas rests on the fact that different approaches to legal reception within the EEC were one of the overarching problems which was solved by attaining legal integration. Can the same be done for the Southern African REC?

This research will also be conducted by way of a literature review in which reference will be made to textbooks, case law, statutes, internet sources, scholarly articles and journals.

Chapter 2: Legal integration as a vehicle for regional economic integration

2.1 Introduction

REI is an economic phenomenon that will be discussed in this chapter. As this research dwells on the legal obstacles that detract from the completion of the REI process, there is a need first to establish the relationship between REI and the law. This will then lead to a discussion of the legal challenge that comes with REI, which is that there are different approaches to legal reception among member states in a REC.

However, this challenge can be understood only if legal reception is defined and the legal theories relating to it are fully explained and compared to illustrate their differences. The proposed solution of legal integration will be fully expounded by clearly laying out how it could be a means to overcome the problem caused by the different approaches to legal reception

Since REI was conceived in Europe, a legal perspective on REI within the EEC will be given. This chapter seeks to identify how the EEC was able to overcome the legal barrier arising from the existence of the different approaches to legal reception among its members. Was legal integration considered as a vehicle for REI in the EEC? If so, how did the EEC attain legal integration?

2.2 The concepts of REI and legal integration in international law

REI has been defined as:[21]

> The co-ordinating of economic activities with the aim of enhancing the development of countries or regions. It involves the elimination of tariff and non -tariff barriers to the flow of goods, services and factors of production between a group of nations, or different parts of the same nation.

---

21 UNECA Report *Assessing Regional Integration in Africa*. ECA policy research report 2004.

REI is a concept that developed post-World War Two in Europe Different member states within the same geographical area were clustered together to form a community that would work towards attaining the economic and socio-political growth of the region.[22] Balassa considers REI as a process and as a state of affairs.[23] He describes the process as taking place in the following stages:

(a) Stage 1- Free Trade Area[24]

(b) Stage 2- Customs Union[25]

(c) Stage 3- Common Market[26]

(d) Stage 4- Economic Union[27]

(e) Stage 5- Complete Economic Integration[28]

While the above stages are the most common stages followed in the establishment of most RECs, they can be applied in the order member states agree to. There is no hard and fast rule about which of these stages must come first. In this light Hailu states:[29]

> While many of the regional integration schemes in the world are based on such formulation, the Balassan stages are not necessarily expected to be pursued with

---

22 Consider the Establishment of the ESCS and the EEC.

23 The economist Balassa describes economic integration in *The theory of Economic Integration* as follows: "We propose to define economic integration as a process and as a state of affairs. Regarded as a process, it encompasses measures designed to abolish discrimination between economic units belonging to different national states; viewed as a state of affairs, it can be represented by the absence of various forms of discrimination between national economies." 1.

24 Balassa *The theory of Economic Integration.* "Tariffs and quantitative restrictions between the participating countries are abolished, but each country retains its own tariffs against non-member states."2.

25 Balassa *The Theory of Economic Integration.* "Establishing a customs union involves, besides the suppression of discrimination in the field of commodity movements within the union, the equalization of tariffs in trade with non-member countries."2.

26 Balassa *The theory of economic integration* "A higher form of economic integration is attained in a common market, where not only trade restrictions but also restrictions on factor movements are abolished."2.

27 Balassa *The Theory of Economic Integration* "An economic union, as distinct from a common market, combines the suppression of restrictions on commodity and factor movements with some degree of harmonization of national economic policies, in order to remove discrimination that was due to disparities in these policies."2.

28 Balassa *The Theory of Economic Integration* "Finally total economic integration presupposes the unification of monetary, fiscal, social, and countercyclical policies and requires the setting up of a supranational authority whose decisions are binding for the member states."2.

29 Hailu 2014 Mizan.L.Rev.

sequential rigidity and there is no compelling reason to expect a FTA to evolve into a CU or toward total economic integration.

2.2.1 Is REI governed by international law?

The process of REI is spearheaded by the signing of treaty agreements by member states, which set out the norms and manner in which the community will function. These treaties have been described as constitutive treaties. Hartley asserts:[30]

> The constitutive treaties lay the foundations of the community, they may be regarded as the constitution of the community, and they set up the various organs of the community and grant them their powers. They also contain many provisions of a non-institutional nature which would not normally be found in a constitution...Appended to many of these treaties there are certain supplementary instruments and annexures and protocols are an integral part of the treaty to which they relate.

It is the signing of these constitutive treaties that has led to the emergence of community law. Community law is a form of international law which has a supranational character.[31] Fagboyibo comments:[32]

> Essentially supranationalism implies the existence of an organisation capable of exercising authoritative powers over its member states. This is the point where supranational organisations are different from inter-governmental institutions, since the latter are merely forums for inter-state cooperation.

The supranational quality of community law has altered the general understanding of international law. There has been much debate amongst international law scholars about whether community law must be considered as a form of international law, considering

---

30 Hartley TC The foundations of European Community Law.

31 Hay P 1965 U.III.L.F 733 "Economic integration in post-war Europe has created a new organizational form for the co-operation and association of states. Described as 'supranational"' these organisations possess both independence from and power over their constituent states to a degree which suggests the emergence of a new federal hierarchy and which goes far beyond traditional intergovernmental cooperation in the form of international organisations".733.

32 Fagbayibo 2013 PER 33; Pescatore in his book *The law of integration* defines supranationality as: "The recognition by a group of member states of a complex of common interests, or more broadly, a complex of common values; the creation of an effective power placed at the service of these interests or values, finally, the autonomy of this power." 50; Sodipe and Osuntogun 2013 PER: "The reality is that even when an organisation possesses all of the elements of supranationalism, there are still some embedded features of inter-governmentalism". 271.

its *sui generis* character that is distant from the general understanding of international law.[33] Marquis has made the following observation:[34]

> From a legal standpoint, the institutional structure of a community raises the question of whether the treaties should be interpreted narrowly, as classic international law requires, or treated as constitutional documents and given a broad characterization.

Marquis believes that the traditional approach of international law must be maintained, and that community law has created a new legal order.[35] On the other hand Verdross is of the opinion that it is not viable for community law to be considered distinct from international law. Rather it must be thought of as a component of international law. He states:[36]

> Either we place the new concept of the "internal law of a community of states" *apart* from the concept of international law (if one wants, like Alf Roos, to restrict the concept of international law, leads to the dissolution of the original mixed concept of international law exclusively to the rules regulating the relations between sovereign legal communities); or -and this is, by far, better-one must adopt a wider concept of international law and then distinguish these two groups within the concept of international law. Such expansion, justified by the historical development of the traditional concept law. We therefore define international law as the *law of the community of states*.

Hartley also states that:[37]

> The community legal system was created by a set of treaties. It depends for its validity on international law. Ultimately therefore community law is a subsystem of international law. However, if a group of states conclude a set of treaties to govern

---

33 Verdross 1949 Am.J.Int'L 435; Elivira and Pinedo *EC and EEA Law:* "Despite being based on treaties drawn up in accordance with international law, community law has increasingly distanced itself from international law. The fundamental reason for this evolution lies in the differing objectives of the two legal orders: whereas international law relates to the resolution of conflicts in law between states, community law is designed to promote integration between its member states and furthermore to create direct effects by directly conferring rights and imposing obligations on individual and enterprises within the member states. For this reason, EC law is frequently defined as *sui-generis* order distinct from, though closely linked to both international law and the laws of the various member states."27.

34 Marquis 1977 J. Int L &Com "By permitting individuals and enterprises to appeal institution decisions, the EEC treaty makes a significant departure from traditional international law, which has generally permitted only states to sue". 210; Hay P 1965 UIII.L. F 741 "Attempts to give content to the *sui generis* concept have resulted in new terms of art: that community law is the 'internal law of the community of states" (*internes Staatengemeinschafts-recht* –Verdoss).

35 Marquis Legal Integration in the Common Market.

36 Verdross 1949 Am.J.Int'L 438.

37 Hartley TC *The foundations of European Community law* 89.

> their relations with each other in a given area, international law permits them to create a new system of law that is self-contained and separate from international law. The normalities of international law will not necessarily apply within that system.

International law can never be given a narrow approach but must be broad to suit the dynamics of change which takes place in the international legal sphere. When RECs forge their relationships by means of a treaty, they have entered into the arena of international law. The *Vienna Convention on the Law of Treaties* (VCLT) defines a treaty as follows:

> Treaty means international agreements concluded between states in written form and governed by international law whether embodied in a single instrument or in two or more instruments or in two or more related instruments and whatever its particular designation.[38]

As long as a treaty is the basis for an agreement, it will be governed by international law despite its uniqueness. The unique feature of such a treaty does not render it impossible for one to assert it as international law. Community law is a form of international law, although unique. For the purposes of REI, international law of a supranational nature is the driving force which drives the REI agenda forward. Even economists such as Balassa state:[39]

> Finally, total economic integration presupposes the unification of monetary, fiscal, social, and countercyclical policies and requires the setting up of a supra-national authority whose decisions are binding for the member states.

For the purposes of REI, it is essential to depart from the main understanding of international law and adopt a supranational authority so as to fully realise REI. However, the fact that community law has adopted a different approach from the traditional understanding of international law does not *perse* ultimately divorce community law from international law. REI and international law can never be divorced from each other.

---

38 A 2 Vienna Convention on the Law of Treaties. (1969).

39 Balassa *The Theory of Economic Integration*. 2.

2.2.2 Legal integration as a means to achieve REI

Consistency in the application of treaties and all protocols relating to regional economic blocs is the essential starting point for the successful realisation of REI in totality. To enable such a foundation to be laid there is a need for the application of such laws emanating from the REC to be uniformly applied by the member states in their own municipal laws.[40] The means to achieve uniformity is by means of legal integration. Mancuso defines legal integration as follows:[41]

> Legal integration is a legal technique aimed at eliminating differences between national provisions by replacing them with a unique and identical text for all states involved.

Political scholars have acknowledged that the process to achieve uniformity of the laws is through legal integration. They define legal integration as follows:[42]

> By legal integration, our dependant variable, we mean the gradual penetration of EC law into the domestic law of its member states. This process has two principal dimensions. First is the dimension of formal penetration, the expansion of the types of supranational legal acts, from treaty law to secondary community law, that takes precedence over domestic law. Second is the dimension of substantive penetration, the spilling over of community legal regulation from the narrowing economic domain into areas dealing with issues such as occupational health, safety, social welfare, education and even political participation rights.

Oppong supports these points and explains the importance of legal integration for the purposes of REI:[43]

> ...effective economic integration is the product of properly structuring and managing, within well–defined legal frameworks, vertical, horizontal and vertico- horizontal relations among states, legal systems, laws and institutions. In other words, a community must have well-structured and managed relations between itself and other legal systems as a necessary condition for its effectiveness.

---

40 Mancuso 2011 *J.Comp.L* 146.
41 Mancuso 2011 *J.Comp.L* 148.
42 Burley and Mattli 1993 *IO* 41.
43 Oppong *Legal Aspects of Economic Integration in Africa*. 31.

Within the domain of interstate cooperation, it is prudent for the legal foundations of the REC to be consistent and to portray a united approach in the manner in which the policies, treaties and protocols are interpreted and applied. Pitarakis and Tridmas have suggested:

> A reliable legal system adds credibility to private economic exchanges enforces contracts, protects economic freedoms and reins in arbitrary state power. It secures that no individual, in either private or public capacity, places itself above the law, protects agents from arbitrary decisions and reduces economic uncertainty.[44]

At this point one can note that the disciplines of law, economics and politics agree on the need for legal integration and how it can be attained by having a supranational body that ensures the consistent application of REI laws. Consistency and certainty lead to economic certainty, which marks successful REI.

However, because of the diverse legal cultures that permeate various RECs, it has been difficult for most of them to successfully ensure the uniform application of REI laws. The process of legal reception in any particular state is wholly determined by that state's municipal laws.

2.3 Defining legal reception

Legal reception is the term used to determine how international law is transplanted into municipal law. As already said, RECs are governed by international law under community law. It is imperative to understand how all treaties, protocols and rules relating to RECs are being transplanted into the municipal laws of the member states.[45] Barnard states:[46]

> The importation of international law into national legal systems relates directly to the question of legal reception. Legal reception relates to the relationship between international and domestic law in that it prescribes how international law should apply within a national legal system.

At the centre of this inquiry international law scholars have from time to time resorted to the monist theory and the dualist theory to determine how the above laws will be transplanted into the municipal laws of states. Oppong states: "Traditionally scholars posit

---

44 Pitarakis and Tridmas 2003 *EJLE* 360.
45 See para 2.2.1 above.
46 Barnard 2015 *CILSA* 154.

two approaches to the reception of international law into the national legal system, characterising countries as monist or dualist."[47] The two theories will give one a clear understanding of the manner in which community law is received within the member states' municipal laws. Ferreira and Snyman state:[48]

> The dichotomy between monism and dualism is no longer relevant to only the relationship between public international law (including regional law) and municipal law, but since the development of regional organisations such as the European Union, it also exerts an influence on the relationship between public international law and regional law.

The two theories relate not only to international law only but also to regional economic blocs. The legal culture inherent within a state's municipal legal order is the determining factor which indicates which theory applies in that state's municipal laws. Countries that conform to the civil law culture follow the monist theory and common law countries follow the dualist theory.[49] Some states adopt the two approaches simultaneously to follow a hybrid system. It is at the heart of this research to clearly evaluate the three theories in the context of REI and how each approach impacts upon the realisation of REI. Giving a detailed description of each of these theories should help to suggest which system would make it easiest to attain legal integration for the ultimate goal of completing the REI process.

2.3.1 Monism

The monist theory became predominant after the First World War.[50] Cassese states:[51]

> The Kelsinian, monist theory, an admirable theoretical construction, was in advance of its time. In many respects it was utopian and did not reflect the reality of international relations. However, for all its inconsistencies and practical pitfalls, it had a significant ideological impact. It brought new emphasis to the role of international law as a controlling factor of state conduct. It was instrumental in consolidating the

---

47 Oppong 2007 *Fordham Int'l L.* J 297; Killander and Adjolohoun. *International Law and Domestic Human Rights.* The relationship between international law and domestic law is often portrayed in terms of the monism dualism dichotomy. African civil law countries have been seen as monist and common law countries as dualist."4.

48 Ferreira and Snyman 2014 *PELJ* 1472.

49 Killander and Ajolohoun "International law and domestic human rights Litigation."

50 Cassese International *law.* "Internationalist monism was propounded as a fully-fledged doctrine after the First World War, between 1920 and 1934, by the Austrian H. Kelsen and was subsequently embraced by a number of distinguished scholars including A Verdross and G. Scelle." 164.

51 Casesse International law.

> notion that state officials should abide by international legal standards and ought therefore to put international imperatives before national demands.

This theory has made international law readily acceptable in civil law countries, which invoke the direct applicability and the supremacy of international law over municipal law.[52]

2.3.2 Dualism

Conversely, dualism considers international law and municipal law as two different legal systems which can never be placed on the same footing.[53]Oppong sets out the dualist theory clearly when he states:[54]

> From a dualist perspective, international law, especially treaty law, cannot claim to be directly part of, let alone superior to, national law. National courts can refuse to apply or put their own varying interpretations on international law. They are under no obligation to seek clarification either from the international organization that adopted the law or the institution that was established by it. Individuals cannot have any directly enforceable rights-or directly imposed duties- under international law, except those expressly created or imposed by national law. In other words, even though rights and responsibilities can be created for individuals at the international level, they remain ineffective at the national level unless they are so recognised under national law...In summary; within many states, foreign and international law enjoy no autonomous or privileged status.

The dualist theory in this instance gives international law a subservient position and subjects it to the laws and principles of the municipal courts.

The monist and dualist theories have divergent views about the principles of international law. These differences are highlighted in the table on the following page:

---

52 Cassesse *International law*: "Thus in France treaties acquire a status higher than national ordinary legislation with the obvious consequences that, in case of conflict, the former prevails." 164.

53 Sloss "Treaty enforcement in Domestic Courts": "Dualists believe that domestic law and international law are independent legal systems."6.

54 Oppong *Legal Aspects of Economic Integration* 33.

Table 2-1: Differences between monism and dualism[55]

Fundamental Principles	Monism	Dualism
Direct applicability[56]	-Immediate application of international agreements within the member states' municipal laws, without the need to follow the municipal law's parliamentary processes of enacting law.	-International agreements do not directly apply in member states' municipal laws. -For member states' obligations to arise from an international agreement they need to follow the process of enacting such an agreement as provided for in the member states' municipal constitution. This is based on parliamentary sovereignty.
Supremacy	-In instances where there is conflict between a municipal law and an international agreement, the international agreement must prevail.[57] -This is influenced by the principle of *pacta sunt servanda,*[58]where states cannot invoke their municipal laws as a means of offending the rules and obligations of international agreements.	-Where there is conflict between the municipal law and an international agreement, municipal law must prevail. -This is conditioned by the norm that legislation is to be obeyed.
Sovereignty	-Member states' sovereignty is not absolute. Especially in instances where states have entered into the arena of community law they have surrendered a part of their sovereignty.	-The sovereignty of member states is absolute. A state may derogate from an international obligation as long as it serves the interest of its sovereignty.

Judicial Sovereignty	-Member states' courts have no absolute judicial sovereignty. -They must consult with international courts or regional courts in matters concerning the application and interpretation of international agreements.	-Member states' courts are not subject to international courts' or regional courts' manner of the application and interpretation of international agreements. -Member states must apply international agreements in a manner that conforms to their municipal laws.
Direct effect	-Natural or juristic persons have the right to be heard before an international or regional court.	-Natural or juristic persons have no right to appear before an international or regional court, because international law governs social relations between states and states alone. This stems from the principle of *Jus inter potestates.*[59] -If natural or juristic persons have concerns pertaining to the application or enforcement of an international or regional agreement they must seek redress in their own municipal courts.

55 Author 's own table

56 Pescatore "Interpretation of Community Law". "It signifies that community rules are endowed with the same kind of effectiveness as national legal rules. Community rules may be directly invoked. It may be affirmed that member states have to admit community laws as being part of the law of the land." 29.

57 Pinedo and Elvira EC and EEA Law 52.

58 Kunz 1945 *Am J'Int L.*: "Undoubtedly a positive norm of general international law". This means that states cannot invoke the legal procedures of their municipal systems as a justification for non-compliance with international rules.

59 Latin term which translates as "law governing relations among sovereign entities."

2.3.3 The hybrid theory

Sloss has correctly stated that some countries do not fit in either the monist category or the dualist category.[60] The harmonisation theory usually applies in states which determine the source of law. If the source of international law is customary international law, then such laws will directly apply within the municipal legal order, as in the monist system.

Whereas, if the source of international law is a treaty, there is a need for such a treaty to be subjected to the constitutional provisions of the municipal legal system of such a state for it to have force and effect within the state. South Africa is one of the Southern African countries that have adopted the harmonisation theory with reference to international law. Customary international law[61] and self–executing treaties in South Africa accede to the monist theory, whereas general treaties accede to the dualist theory.[62] The application of these theories had a great influence on the manner in which the EEC laws were to be incorporated within EEC member states' municipal laws.

2.4 REI in the European context

REI in Europe emerged when the European Coal and Steel and Community (ESCS) was formed under the *Treaty establishing the European Coal and Steel and Community* (*Treaty of Paris*). After seven years it led to the formation of the European Economic Community (EEC), which was established under the *Treaty establishing the European Economic Community* (*Treaty of Rome*).[63] The *Treaty of Rome* clearly outlined the REI process, setting one of its main objectives to be the integration of the economies of the member states, under article 2, which reads:[64]

---

60 Sloss "Treaty enforcement in Domestic Courts": "Although the scholars use the terms monist and dualist to describe different types of domestic legal systems, the actual legal systems of many states do not fit neatly into either of these two categories." Germany, The Netherlands, Poland, Russia, South Africa and the United States hybridise the theories.7.

61 See the detailed discussion in Chapter 4 of this research on Section 232 of the *Constitution of the Republic of South Africa* ,1996.

62 Section 231(4).

63 *Treaty of Rome* signed on the 25th of March 1957 and entered into force on the 1st of January 1958. Article 1 reads: "By this treaty, the high contracting parties establish among themselves EEC. Member states included: Belgium, Denmark, Germany, France, Ireland, Italy, Luxembourg, Netherlands, and United Kingdom.

64 A 2 *Treaty of Rome.*

> The community shall have as its task, by establishing a common market and progressively approximating the economic policies of member states to promote throughout the community a harmonious development of economic activities, a continuous and balanced expansion, and an increase in stability, an accelerated raising of the standard of living and closer relations between the states belonging to it.

The EEC was able to progress throughout the five stages of REI which marked the establishment of the European Union. Moghadam considers the establishment of the EU to be the heart of integration. He states:[65]

> While Europe is much larger and more populous than the European Union alone, the union has been at the heart of European Integration, binding countries once in conflict and offering benefits well beyond its borders- as a key trading and investment partner across Europe and as a powerful catalyst for fundamental economic governance reforms by many entrants and aspirants.

The completion of the REI process yielded many economic benefits for Europe, which included high levels of Foreign Direct Investment (FDI) and "great bargaining power due to the increased market size of the integrated states".[66] On the other hand this does not mean that the REI process in Europe did not have its own obstacles. As mentioned earlier, in this research emphasis will be placed on the legal obstacles which the EEC had to overcome, in particular the different approaches to legal reception and how they impacted upon the realisation of REI. This necessitates an examination of legal reception during the formation of the EEC, and how the challenges attached to legal reception were overcome within the EEC.

2.4.1 Legal reception in the EEC

When the EEC was formed, the member states had various legal cultures, which meant that they had various means to legal reception. The manner in which they received classical international law within their own municipal legal systems was a key indicator of how EEC laws would be recognised within member states' municipal laws. The table below shows the founding member states of the EEC and which system relating to legal reception the member states practised within their own municipal laws.

---

65 Moghadam 2014 http://www.imf.org.

66 Hancock *Regional Integration* 29.

Table 2-2 An overview of EEC member states approach to legal reception[67]

Member states	Monism	Dualism
Belgium	✓	
Denmark		✓
France	✓	
Germany		✓
Italy		✓
Ireland		✓
Luxembourg	✓	
Netherlands	✓	
United Kingdom		✓

Of the nine member states of the EEC, five followed the dualist approach when it came to the reception of international law within their own municipal laws. Only three countries were exclusively monist, as shown above: France, Netherlands and Luxembourg.

Figure 2-1: Legal reception in the EEC[68]

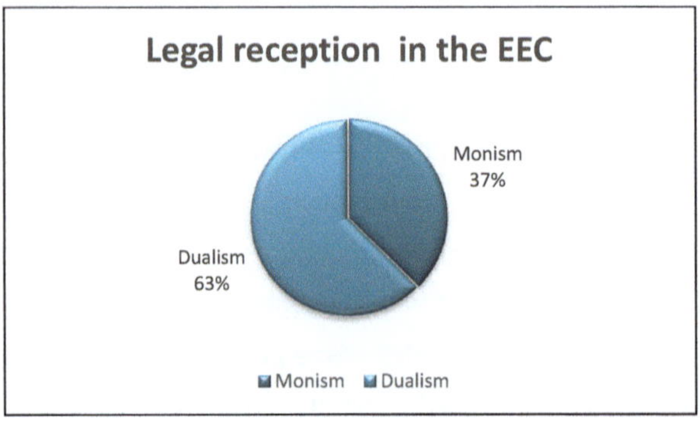

67 Author's own table; Ciongaru 2012 *UGBJ* 213-232.

68 Author's own pie chart.

Sixty-three percent of the EEC member states followed the dualist approach pertaining to the reception of international law. This meant that international law did not directly apply within the member states' municipal laws. The member states had absolute sovereignty, and natural or juristic persons did not have access to international courts. This approach would apply to EEC laws, a fact which would strain the uniform reception and implementation of the laws and the completion of the REI process within Europe. Legal reception was a barrier to the success of the EEC but the member states managed to surmount it. The important question to ask is how the EEC managed to ensure that the EEC laws applied uniformly within the entire community and had the same force and effect, thus ensuring certainty

2.4.2 Facets of legal integration in the EEC

Legal integration has proven to be the means of directing the process of REI in full within the European context. It made it possible to overcome the legal barrier of the existence of different approaches to legal reception.

2.4.2.1 Judicial arm as the driving force to legal integration

Burley and Mattli state:[69]

> The European Court of Justice has been the dark horse of European integration, quietly transforming the Treaty of Rome into a European Community (EC) constitution and steadily increasing the impact and scope of EC law. While legal scholars have tended to take the court's power for granted, political scientists have overlooked it entirely.

The judicial arm should never be underestimated when in relation to the realisation of REI in Europe. The European Court of Justice (ECJ) was the main driving force that acted as the guardian of the *Treaty of Rome*.[70] It derived its powers from the *Treaty of Rome,* which provided under article 164: "The court of justice shall ensure that in the

---

69 Barley and Mattli 1993 *IO* 41.

70 Tam "The history of the Court of Justice" has stated: "For the historian, there is nothing surprising in the fact that the court actually took advantage of the legal possibilities offered by the European treaties to further the project once it was started on a less ambitious scale." 12.

interpretation and application of this treaty the law is observed."[71]Kelman and Schmidt also state: "The European Court of Justice (ECJ) has played an indispensable role as a motor for European Integration."[72] It ensured that its decisions would lead to the uniform application of and consistency in all protocols related to REI.

Article 4 of the *Treaty of Rome* gave the ECJ the mandate to ensure that the member states implemented and adhered to the provisions of the treaty.[73]Pescatore[74] considers this to be the doctrine of effective power whereby the ECJ would take decisions which were binding on the states.[75] The decisions of the ECJ pertaining to the *Treaty of Rome* reigned supreme over decisions made by the member states' municipal courts. This signalled that municipal courts no longer had absolute judicial sovereignty but instead yielded their decisions pertaining to the *Treaty of Rome* to a higher authority, which was the ECJ. The ECJ was empowered to interfere with the laws of member states by means of article 177 of the *Treaty of Rome,* which reads:

> The court of justice shall have jurisdiction to give preliminary rulings concerning:
> (a) The interpretation of this treaty.
> (b) The validity and interpretation of acts of the institutions of the community.
> (c) The interpretation of the statutes of bodies established by an act of the council where these statutes so provide.

Where such a question is raised before any court or tribunal of a member state, that court or tribunal may, if it considers that a decision on the question is necessary to enable it to give judgement, request the court of justice to give a ruling thereon. In this regard the highest court of the member states' municipal laws had to consult with the ECJ before making any ruling that concerned the implementation of the *Treaty of Rome*. In England the courts stated in *R v Secretary of State for transport Ex p Factortame Ltd*:[76]

> If we say that sovereignty means the ability to legislate independently of any other state, if it means that our domestic laws will prevail over all other external laws, then the UK long gave up some of its sovereignty.

---

71 A 177 of the *Treaty of Rome*.

72 Kelemen and Schmidt 2011 *J' E, P, P* 1.

73 A 4 of the *Treaty of Rome* reads:" The task entrusted to the community shall be carried out by the following institutions: The court of justice. Europe before the court."

74 Pescatore Law of Integration.51.

75 Pescatore *Law of Integration*: To take decisions which are binding on states, to lay down rules of law which they must respect, to pronounce judicial decisions, determining the law, these are the kind of powers which go into the making of a supranationality. 51.

76 No (7) (2001).

The negative effect of article 177 of the *Treaty of Rome* was that member states yielded their judicial sovereignty as a means of ensuring that legal integration was achieved for REI to be realised. However, this was necessary, as Marquis points out:[77]

> Referral Jurisdiction is essential to achieve uniformity in the interpretation of community law. Lack of uniformity could well lead to community law being ignored, an occurrence which would undermine the viability of the community. The solution to the problem of the interrelationship between community law and municipal law depends in large measures upon referral jurisdiction.

The means to which the ECJ would ensure consistency of the law in the EEC was by keeping track of the manner in which the laws were interpreted within the municipal courts, so that a united approach to all legal issues would be followed within the EEC. Pescatore discusses the issue as follows:[78]

> Community law must have the same substantive meaning wherever they are applied. The procedure of preliminary rulings in the communities has proved to be the most practical means for settling controversies rapidly and eliminating distortions about the meaning of common rules... what matters is not only unity of content but also uniformity of validity and efficacy. In fact, the disturbance to the functioning of the communities would be much greater if the same rules did not have, in the different member countries, the same kind of effect. The fact that certain rules would be effectively applied in some member countries, whereas in others their implementation would be hampered or even rendered impossible, would have a much more disruptive effect on the community system. This raises a problem of efficacy.

The preliminary rulings of the ECJ ensured a satisfactory degree of unanimity in the interpretation of the community laws, and this led to legal certainty, which in turn resulted in economic certainty. There was some resistance from some member states pertaining to the use of the preliminary rulings, however.[79]

2.4.2.2 Supremacy of the *Treaty of Rome*

Bearing in mind that they are two different types of laws within the EEC, which are the municipal laws of the member states and the community laws, often the municipal courts

---

77 Marquis 1978 *J.INt.L& Com* 212.

78 Pescatore "Interpretation of Community Law and the Doctrine of *Acte Clair*" 30.

79 Marquis 1978 *J.Int.L& Com* France, Italy and Germany.223.

and the ECJ have had to address the problem of the conflict between the two systems: which laws prevail over which? In France the Court of Cassation in the *Ramel Case* provided: "The treaties and binding community acts have an authority superior to the French laws."[80] The Belgian courts also emphasized that the types of legal systems involved have different sources of law. In the case of *Minister of Economic affairs v Fromagerie Franco Suisse*[81] the court provided that a national law could never repeal a treaty provision, but a treaty provision can nullify a national law. It stated:

> The rule that a statute repeals a previous statute in so far as there is a conflict between the two does not apply in the case of a conflict between a treaty and a statute. In the event of a conflict between a norm of domestic law and a norm of international law... the rule established by the treaty shall prevail.

From the above one can deduce that the municipal legal order had to be subservient to the community legal order so as to fulfil the provisions of the *Treaty of Rome*, as a means to ensure uniform and consistent application of the law. In Britain, Lord Denning in the case of *MacCarthy v Smith* stated that[82] "...we are entitled to look to the treaty as an aid to its construction and even more, not only as an aid but as an overriding force. It is our bounden duty to give priority to community law."[83]This position was confirmed in the *Factorame case*.[84]

In Germany there was much resistance to the notion of community law being superior to national law. The Frankfurt Administrative Court was against the idea of German basic law being subservient to community law.[85] This matter was referred to the *Internationale Handelsgeselleschaft,* which in turn referred the matter to the ECJ. The ECJ firmly maintained the supremacy of community law over municipal law. Oppong concludes:[86]

> The principle of supremacy should be distinguished from provisions often found in the founding treaties of communities that oblige member states to ensure the conformity of their laws with community law. In theory, such provisions are not conflict of laws

---

80 Case 80/1977.
81 [1972] CMLR 330.
82 [1980] Case 129/79.
83 No (7) (2001).
84 Lord Bridge stated: "The high court now has a duty to take account of and give effect to community law and where there is a conflict, to prefer community law to national law."
85 Marquis 1978 *J.INt.L&Com* 222.
86 Oppong *Legal Aspects of Economic Integration in Africa* 48.

> resolution provisions. They look to the executive and legislature rather than the judiciary for action. Their violation will often be a breach of an international obligation remediable at the international rather than national level. What the principle of supremacy declares is that where national law is not in conformity with community law, national courts should give preference to and apply community law.

Maintaining the supremacy of the EEC laws over municipal laws created certainty and uniformity within the RECs legal sphere, thus enabling legal integration which was key to REI. Ultimately the various jurisdictions came to the understanding that EEC laws were superior to their national laws. Marquis states: "The first ground was the necessity of preventing harm to the unity and efficacy of community law."[87]

2.4.2.3 Limited sovereignty of member states

By means of signing the treaty of Rome the member states to the EEC surrendered some of their powers and limited their sovereignty as a means to ensure that the set objectives of the EEC would be realised. Pescatore[88] describes the distinct nature of community law by pointing out that unlike a situation in an intergovernmental organisation where a member state retains full sovereignty, integration limits member states' sovereignty. He states: "The law of integration rests on a premise quite known to so-called classical 'international law': that of the divisibility of sovereignty."[89]

In *Costa v Enel* the court clearly stated:[90]

> By creating a community of unlimited duration, having its own institutions, its own personality, its own legal capacity and capacity of representation on the international plane, and more particularly, real powers, international standing and more particular real powers stemming from a limitation of sovereignty, or a transfer of powers from the state to the community the member states have limited their sovereign rights, albeit within their limited fields, and have thus created a body of law which binds both their nationals and themselves.,. ... The transfer by the states from their domestic legal system to the community legal order of their rights and obligations arising under the treaty carries with a permanent limitation of their sovereign rights against which a subsequent unilateral act incompatible with the concept of community cannot prevail.

---

87 Marquis 1978 *J.INt.L&Com* 229.

88 Pescatore *Law of integration* 26.

89 Pescatore *Law of integration* "...the preconceived idea of indivisible sovereignty blinds men's minds to the phenomenon of integration." 31.

90 *Costa v Enel* 15 July 1964.

The *Pit face bonus judgement* justified limiting the national sovereignty of member states in community law to whatever extent was necessary to ensure that the objectives of the community were not diminished or compromised.[91] Limited sovereignty was a negative obligation set by the ECJ court so as to realise the purposes of the REI in Europe. Had the member states maintained their prerogative of absolute sovereignty, some of them would have hidden behind the veil of sovereignty as a means of avoiding implementing the rules established by the EEC. As mentioned earlier on there was a need for the uniform application of the treaty as a means to create consistency and certainty, which are the key ingredients of an effective REI. Pescatore states:[92]

> It signifies that community rules are endowed with the same kind of effectiveness as national legal rules. Community rules may be directly invoked ...It thus turns out that through the doctrine of direct application the national judges have been entrusted with the task of implementing, each one in the field of his jurisdiction of the rules of community law.

The limitation of sovereignty was key to realising legal integration, which was a means to REI in the EEC. The role of the ECJ in this regard ensured uniformity of the EEC laws. In the course of making its decisions, it developed concepts such as the limitation of sovereignty and the supremacy of the EEC laws over municipal laws. The *Treaty of Rome* was designed to ensure that the judicial sovereignty of the member states was also limited by way of preliminary rulings. In this regard the EEC was able to embrace its supranational nature as a special kind of legal order and managed to bypass the difficulty of the different systems of legal reception to be found in the municipal laws of different member states. Knowing that sixty-three percent of the member states of the EEC espoused the dualist theory, the ECJ addressed the need to prioritize the EEC laws before all else, regardless of what was prescribed within member states' municipal laws.

---

91 Pescatore *Law of integration* 27. *Gezamenlijke Steenkolenmijnenen* in Limburg.

92 Pescatore "Interpretation of community law and the doctrine of *Acte Clair*" 29.

2.5 Conclusion

The REI phenomenon has been introduced in this chapter by clearly defining what REI is all about. From a legal perspective, the chapter had to determine how REI is related to international law. This made it necessary to expound on the proposition that the law can be used as a means to attain REI, thus bringing about legal integration. At the heart of legal integration lies the need to understand the legal obstacles emanating from the different approaches to legal reception. This chapter has also defined legal reception, the different approaches to legal reception, and the differences between them.

Next it was asked if the law could be used as a means to complete REI, but this had to be done by analysing the different approaches to legal reception within the EEC and establishing how the EEC was able to remove the barrier emanating from such approaches in order to complete the REI process. The role played by the ECJ in this instance was discussed and how the fundamental principles relating to the different theories of legal reception were applied within the EEC by the ECJ itself and the municipal judiciary of member states within the EEC. It has been established that legal integration is a plausible solution for the problems that attend on the different approaches to legal reception.

Chapter 3: The approach to legal reception by Southern African RECs

3.1 Introduction

In Africa, REI is to be achieved at sub regional level.[93] In Southern Africa there are two sub-regional groupings which will serve as the primary focus of this chapter. These are the SADC and the COMESA

Not much is being done within the SADC to ensure the completion of the REI process. Twenty-three years have passed since the SADC was formed, but it has managed to complete only the first stage of the REI process, which is establishing a FTA.[94] The COMESA has reached the second stage of REI, which is establishing the Customs Union.[95] Judging from COMESA's Medium Term Strategic Plan (MTSP), it is expected that COMESA's common market will soon be established.

The SADC's Regional Indicative Strategic Development Plan (RISDP) has reiterated the need to bring all legal frameworks pertaining to trade and the SADC as a whole in uniformity. This goes to show that legal integration is considered as a strategy to realise REI. The MTSP clearly asserts that the key to REI is mutual beneficial cooperation. Cooperation also relates to ensuring that the COMESA laws are in uniformity, thus creating certainty within the REC.

The member states of the two regional groupings in Southern Africa have different approaches to legal reception. This chapter seeks to evaluate how the different approaches to legal reception by member states in Southern Africa impact upon the realisation of REI.

---

93 A 88 of the *Abuja Treaty*.

94 Balassa *The Theory of Economic Integration*. "Tariffs and quantitative restrictions between the participating countries are abolished, but each country retains its own tariffs against non-member states." 2.

95 Balassa *The Theory of Economic Integration*. "Establishing a customs union involves, besides the suppression of discrimination in the field of commodity movement's within the union, the equalization of tariffs in trade with non-member countries." 2.

This chapter seeks to give a brief history of REI in Arica. It goes on to discuss legal reception in Southern Africa and its impact on REI by looking into the two existing RECs in Southern Africa. Are the different approaches to legal reception by the two RECs one of the causes why it is taking a long time to complete REI in the SADC? If so, how are the different approaches to legal reception delaying the REI process? Can the same be said for COMESA? Are the different approaches to legal reception in COMESA an obstacle to the realisation of REI?

3.2 REI in Africa

In Africa, the REI process was initiated at the continental level by the founding members of the OAU.[96] The 1979 Monrovia Declaration[97] set the tone; heads of states of the OAU vowed to effectively involve themselves in the process of REI. They vowed to ensure effective REI at municipal level and continental level.[98] A close examination of the Monrovia Declaration shows that the Pan-African leaders fully acknowledged the need for a collective effort to realise economic growth for the good of the African people.[99] The declaration opens with the following:

> Determined to ensure that our member states individually and collectively restructure their economic and social strategies and programmes so as to achieve rapid socio-economic change and to establish a solid domestic and intra African base for a self-sustaining, self-reliant development and economic growth...[100]

Mere declaration was not sufficient to impel the realisation of REI in Africa. The member states of the OAU set out a two-decade plan on how economic development in Africa was to be realised. The Lagos Plan of Action for the Economic Development of Africa, 1980–

---

96 See para 1.1.

97 Resolution NO:AHG/ST.3(XXI) Monorovia Declaration of commitment of the heads of state and Government of the Organisation of African Unity on guidelines and measures for national and collective self–reliance in social and economic development for the establishment of a New international Economic Order.

98 "The term declaration is used for various international instruments. However, declarations are not always legally binding. The term is often deliberately chosen to indicate that the parties do not intendtocreatebindingobligationsbutmerelywanttodeclarecertainobligations.http://treaties.un.org/overview.aspx?pcth=overview/definition/page1-en.xml.

99 See par 1.1.

100 The first declaration reads: "Hereby Declares(1)That we commit ourselves individually and collectively on behalf of our governments and peoples to promote the social and economic development and integration of our economies' development and integration of our economies with a view of achieving and increasing measures of self-reliance and self-sustainment."

2000(Lagos Plan of Action) detailed how the member states were to see to it that REI was achieved.1980-1990 was declared the industrial development decade in Africa.[101] In relation to trade and finance,[102] member states were required to eliminate any trade barriers or obstacles slowing the achievement of REI.[103]

However, not much was done to activate the REI process by the member states of the OAU. The Organisation was ineffective in fulfilling the REI agenda.[104] The only tangible achievements made by the OAU were in the political sphere, where Africa was decolonised. In 1990 the approach to REI was reconsidered, which initiative saw the beginning of the implementation of REI at a sub–regional level.

3.2.1 Abuja Treaty: establishing the mandate for REI at sub-regional level

The *Treaty Establishing the African Economic Community*[105] (*Abuja Treaty*) came into effect in 1990, ten years after the member states of the OAU had made declarations about founding an African Economic Community (AEC). The *Abuja Treaty* requires that every member state of the Organisation of African Unity (OAU) respect the law of the African community.

The parties to the *Abuja Treaty* undertook to do everything in their power to ensure that REI would succeed, as was provided under article 5(1) of the *Abuja Treaty*. A close examination of the principles set out in the *Abuja Treaty* show that the law was considered to be a means to effect the provisions of the Monrovia declarations and the Lagos Plan of Action. Article 3 of the *Abuja Treaty* reads:

> The high contracting parties, in pursuit of the objectives stated in article 4 of this treaty, solemnly affirm and declare their adherence to the following principles:

---

101 Chapter II of the Lagos Plan of Action: Industry reads: Member states accord, in their development plans, a major role to industrialisation, in view of its impact on meeting the basic needs of the population, ensuring the integration of the economy and the modernisation of society...Member states proclaim the years 1980 to 1990 Industrial Development Decade in Africa.

102 Chapter IV II Trade and Finance.

103 (e) Member states should endeavour to eliminate all obstacles which have the effect of curtailing trade among themselves by the year 1990.

104 Fagbayibo 2011 *SAYIL* "The view was held that the organisation had completed its primary functions namely, eradicating colonialism, ending apartheid and establishing the independence of African states".213.

105 (1991).

(a) Interstate co-operation, harmonisation of policies, integration of programmes;
(b) Promotion of harmonious development of economic activities among member states;
(c) Observance of the legal system of the community;
(d) Accountability, economic justice and popular participation in development.

However, the mandate to integrate the legal framework was incumbent upon the RECs. Article 88(1) of the *Abuja Treaty* clearly leaves the RECs to be the main building blocks of the REI process in Africa. This is materially correct, but the signatories to the *Abuja Treaty* were not the RECs themselves but instead were different member states of the REC. Creating a mandate for an REC of which they are not members does not directly oblige them to ensure that REI is achieved at a sub-regional level, simply because there is no consent, express or implied, in such a relationship. Saurombe states:[106]

> The RECs should also be made signatories to the Abuja Treaty. This will require that the RECs be allowed to negotiate terms that reflect their various stages of development and the rate at which they can afford to move. This is necessary so that member states and RECs can be held accountable for failure to honour the Abuja Treaty obligations.

What article 88 of the *Abuja Treaty* does is to merely state an aspiration which is of no force and effect, because there was no direct involvement of the RECs in their own capacity. In this regard the need for legal integration is misdirected to the wrong parties.

3.2.2 Re-birth of the mandate for REI in Africa

A clean slate upon which the member states could inscribe how they intended to achieve economic integration was crucial for the continent. This saw the emergence of the Sirte Declaration.[107] The member states in this regard had to reconsider the approach that had been followed to effect REI. A sense of urgency to implement the REI agenda can be noted, considering that after the 1980 Lagos Plan of Action the drive for REI became

---

106 Saurombe 2012 *SAPL*.

107 Sitre Declaration of 1999 EAhg/Draft 1Dec (IV) Rex at the fourth extra ordinary session of the assembly of heads of states and governments. Declaration 6 reads: "It is also our conviction that our continental organisation needs to be revitalised in order to be able to play a more active role and continue to be relevant to the needs of our peoples and responsive to the demands of the prevailing circumstances. We are also determined to eliminate the scourge of conflicts, which constitutes a major impediment to the implementation of our development and integration agenda".

legally binding when the *Abuja Treaty* came into play. The decade of waiting stalled the economic integration process. The leaders declared in that they wanted to:[108]

> (8) Accelerate the process of implementing the treaty establishing the African Economic community in particular.
> (a) Shorten the implementation period of the Abuja Treaty.

Declarations such as the Sirte declaration can be seen as a formal admission of the aspirations that the member states sought to fulfil. They concretised these aspirations, bound themselves and formally laid out the mandate for REI by signing the *Constitutive Act of the African Union* (*AU Constitutive Act*).[109] The parties to the treaty saw the need to act speedily to see to it that the agenda for effective economic integration was realised as had been contemplated in the Sirte Declaration.[110]

The AU went on to oblige the existing RECs to ensure that they implemented the economic integration plan. The *Protocol on relations between the African Union (AU) and the Regional Economic Communities (REC)*[111] (*Protocol on relations*) determined the mandate which the RECs were to fulfil so as to ensure that REI took place on the sub regional level and that this would eventually lead to establishing the AEC.[112]

The RECs now had the mandate to ensure that economic integration took place within their sub-regional communities. This followed the conciliatory approach that was set in the Sirte Declaration under the provision of article 8(c).[113] This provision shows that the RECs were considered the vehicles that would steer the African economic integration, and may perhaps be seen as a rectification of the exclusion of the RECs from the *Abuja Treaty* framework. Again the protocol's main objective was to urgently implement the provisions

---

108 Sitre Declaration of 1999 EAhg/Draft 1Dec (IV).

109 The act opens with: "Recalling the declaration which we adopted at the fourth Extra–ordinary session of our assembly in Sirte, the great socialists' People's Libyan Arab Jamahiriya, on 9.9.99, in which we decided to establish an African Union, in conformity with the ultimate objectives of the charter of our continental organization and the treaty establishing the African community".

110 A 3 (c) reads: "accelerate the political and social economic integration of the continent".

111 Protocol on relations between the African Union (AU) and the Regional Economic Communities (RECs).

112 A 2 of the protocol provides: "This protocol shall apply to the mechanisms established by the parties in the implementation of measures in the economic, social political and cultural fields including gender, peace and security, intended to fulfil the responsibilities placed on them by the Constitutive Act, the Treaty, and this protocol".

113 A 8(c) reads: "Strengthening and consolidating the RECs as the pillars for achieving the objectives of the AEC and realising the envisaged union.

of the Sirte Declaration, where the RECs had been required to accelerate the integration process.[114]The grass-roots level approach taken by the AU can be seen as a transfer of the mandate of REI to the RECs.

3.3 Legal reception in Southern Africa

Southern Africa contains two RECs, namely the SADC and COMESA.[115] The two RECs are parties to the *Abuja Treaty* and the *Protocol on relations,* which means that they have the mandate to ensure the completion of the REI process within their own RECs. The SADC was formed under the Treaty Establishing the Southern African Development Community (*SADC Treaty*) and one of its main objectives is to achieve development on all fronts by means of REI.[116] The treaty identifies legal integration as the means to fulfil its objectives.[117] On the Other hand, COMESA emerged as a result of the Agreement establishing the Common Market for Eastern and Southern Africa, (*COMESA Treaty*) whose main objectives were to realise harmonious development –thus, REI.[118] The *COMESA Treaty* further provided that in the field of economic and social development there it was necessary to harmonise the laws and policies of its members.[119]

The table below gives an overview of the Southern African member states that belong to the COMESA and the SADC. It also indicates the type of theory which every member state subscribes to when adopting international law within their municipal laws.[120] The information is based on the current constitutional provisions of each member state.

114 A 3(d) of the *Protocol on relations between the African Union (AU) and the Regional Economic Communities (REC's)* reads: "Implement the Sirte Declaration with regard to the acceleration of the integration process and shorten the periods provided for in Article 6 of the treaty".

115 See par 1.1.

116 A 5 (1) (a).

117 A 5 (2) (a).

118 A 3 (a).

119 A 4 (6) (b).

120 See para 2.4.

Table 3-1: Southern Africa's approach to legal reception[121]

Country	SADC	COMESA	Monism	Dualism	Hybrid
Angola	•	•	•		
Botswana	•			•	
DRC	•	•		•	
Lesotho	•			•	
Madagascar	•	•			•
Malawi	•	•		•	
Mauritius	•	•		•	
Mozambique	•		•		
Namibia	•	•			•
South Africa	•				•
Seychelles	•	•			•
Swaziland	•	•		•	
Tanzania	•	•		•	
Zambia	•	•		•	
Zimbabwe	•	•	•		

3.3.1 Historical influences of the dualist theory in Southern Africa

The most predominant theory to determine the status and applicability of community laws within Southern Africa is the dualist theory, as the pie chart below seeks to show. 60% of the Southern African states apply the dualist theory. This is relatively similar to the situation in the EEC at its inception, when sixty-three percent of the founding member states applied the dualist theory within their own municipal laws.[122]

121 Author's own table.
122 See fig 2.1.

To shed the Southern Africa 's approach to legal reception in pictorial form, the pie chart below attempts to lay out Southern Africa's position in the form or percentages based on the different theories that relate to legal reception.

Figure 3-1: Legal reception in Southern Africa[123]

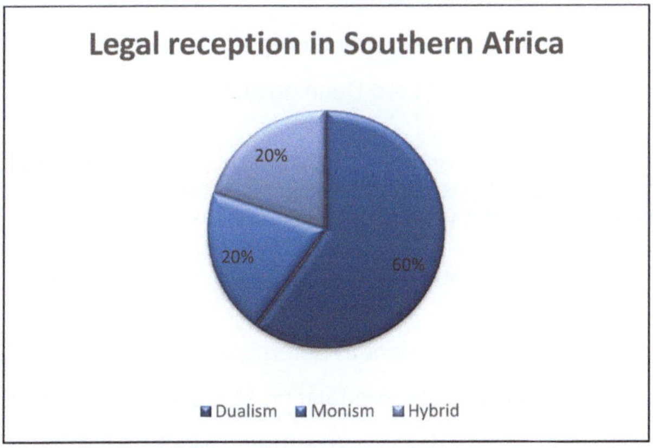

From the above, one can notice that there is not much difference between the EEC and Southern African member states who dominantly apply the dualist theory. As highlighted earlier on 63% of the EEC member states apply the dualist theory,[124] whereas, in Southern Africa 60% apply the dualist theory. when it came to legal reception of international law as highlighted earlier on in Fig 2.1. 20% of the member states follow the monist theory whereas 20% have adopted a hybrid of both theories, as in the case of South Africa, as highlighted earlier on.[125]

The dualist theory is applied in most Southern African states primarily because most Southern African states have inherited the legal cultures of their colonial masters. Britain was the dominant colonial master in Southern Africa, and by its nature is a dualist country. Hartley states:[126]

---

123 Author's own pie chart.
124 See Fig 2.1.
125 See table 3.1.
126 Hartley *The Foundations of European Community law* 261.

> The UK has a largely unwritten constitution Moreover the attitude of the United Kingdom towards international law is strictly dualistic: there is no general rule of law allowing treaties to take effect in the internal legal system. So this route could not be used to give effect to the community treaties.

The dualist theory was applied even when it related to REI under the EEC. The British parliament agreed to the direct applicability of the EEC laws only when it passed a special act known as The *European Communities Act.*[127] This mechanism allowed the parliament to retain its powers including the power to repeal this act when it deemed it necessary to do so. In *Mccarthy v Smith*[128] Lord Denning stated:[129]

> I have assumed that our parliament, whenever it passes legislation, intends to fulfil its obligations under the treaty. If the time should come when our parliament deliberately passes an Act with the intention of repudiating the Treaty...and say so in express terms, then I should have thought that it would be the duty of our courts to follow the statute of our parliament.

It was incumbent upon the parliament to determine if community law would apply. It had the power to decide otherwise by repudiating this act. Ambani is of the view that the powers of the legislature in a dualist system are meant merely to keep the executive's prerogatives in check.[130] Oppong puts the relational powers of the different organs of the state into perspective when he states:[131]

> By giving effect to it (the treaty) absent a national implementing measure, the judiciary may be indirectly setting itself up against the will of an elected branch of government or upsetting the balance of power between the various organs of government. At another level, giving effect to unincorporated treaties indirectly allows the executive to change the law without any intervention from the legislature, which is the law making body. This will unwittingly enhance the powers of the executive at the expense of the legislature by adding indirect law=making power to its competence. As treaties become more important in domestic law, these power relation issues become more prominent in Africa.

Such relational issues have to do with the doctrine of the separation of powers, which plays an important role in determining legal reception. The executive, the legislative and the judiciary have different roles to play in the reception of international law. Signing

---

127 European Communities Act of 1972 Chapter 68.
128 [1980] Case 129/179 ECR 1275.
129 [1980] Case 129/179 ECR 1275.
130 Ambani Navigating past the dualist doctrine 27.
131 Oppong.2007 *Fordham J.Int'L*317.

treaties is an executive prerogative. However, a signed treaty will not become part of municipal law until the legislature enacts it in parliament. The interpretation of the treaty is left to the judiciary.

3.3.2 Dualist theory and sovereignty in Southern Africa

As indicated earlier, in Table 2-1, the dualist theory also relates to state sovereignty. The sovereignty of states requires state approval for another legal system to apply in its own jurisdiction. In this regard Oppong states: [132]

> Because states are sovereign, giving effect to or enforcing a law emanating from another system should often have the express or tacit approval of the state. Where the courts enforce or use foreign laws without this approval, they are accused of inappropriate judicial activism and of blurring the lines between executive, judicial and legislative functions.

However, many states in Africa still grapple with understanding that sovereignty is not absolute and can be limited. Perhaps this intransigence can be attributed to the fact that when most African states fought for independence they envisaged sovereignty and self-determination as key indicators of independence, in which they were in fact correct. However, sovereignty has evolved with time in reaction to the globalisation of many aspects of governance. If at present many African states still assume that they have sovereignty in the traditional sense, this must be because they have not yet embraced the fact that sovereignty is dynamic and not static.

Sovereignty is still thought of as being absolute in respect of internal matters in common law countries that adhere to the dualist theory. Snyman has defined internal sovereignty as "The competence and authority to exercise the function of a state within a national border and to regulate internal affairs freely."[133]

Southern African states are inclined still to embrace internal sovereignty.[134] The International Commission on Intervention and State Sovereignty (ICSS) found that

---

132 Oppong Making REC laws enforceable in national legal systems 157.

133 Snyman *The erosion of state sovereignty in Public International Law* 36.

134 Glednhuys 2012 *AI*.

although states may continue to enjoy absolute sovereignty, this must not lead to them being irresponsible in an international context.

In Seychelles in the matter *Hackl v The Financial Intelligence Unit*[135] the applicant contested the constitutionality of the *Proceeds of Crime Civil Confiscation Act*[136](POCCA) in terms of which the respondent acted by attaching the applicant's financial assets and properties. The respondent had argued that attaching the applicant's property in this regard was justifiable and in the interest of justice, as he had exported components for nuclear war heads to Iran, a country which was under international watch as it had exceeded its uranium levels and was therefore a threat to international security.[137] The applicant dismissed this act as a breach of Seychelles' sovereignty as it was importing criminal offences from other jurisdictions and making them part of Seychelles' legal system. Twomey J stated that the sovereignty of Seychelles could be limited in some circumstances and could not always be absolute. He conceived international obligations arising out of treaty agreements as limiting Seychelles' sovereignty. In this instance the *Treaty on the Non Proliferation of Nuclear Weapons* (NPT) under article 1 prohibited Seychelles from assisting in the manufacturing of nuclear weapons,[138] along with the *United Nations Human Rights Charter* (Human Rights Charter).[139]Twomey J stated:[140]

> We have also had to consider in this context whether there are permissible limitations to the principle of sovereignty. We find that there are. In this context we state that the rule of law and international human rights law may well override a state's claim to sovereignty...The present case concerns the export of components of nuclear warheads and the public, national and international interest far outweighs the principle of sovereignty.

The Seychelles court of appeal in this instance relied on the international law concept of obligations *erga omnes*[141]where it shared a common interest with member states of the NPC and the Human Rights Charter in ensuring its citizens did not partake in the manufacturing of nuclear weapons by supplying material for such a purpose. If it

---

135 (SCA 10 /2011).
136 Act 19 of 2008 POCCA.
137 Council on Foreign Relations 2014 http://www.cfr.org.
138 A 1 of the Treaty on the Non-Proliferation of Nuclear Weapons (1970).
139 A 1of the United Nations Human Rights Charter ((1945).
140 (SCA 10 /2011).Par 14.
141 Vidmar "Norms Conflicts and Hierarchy in International Law" 23.

breached its obligations under the NPT or the Human Rights Charter this would have been an injury to the international community as a whole in its fight against the manufacturing of nuclear weapons.

The Seychelles SCA can be considered to have been seeking to maintain the contractual balance necessary for the accomplishment of common interest.[142] The international interest that limited Seychelles' sovereignty emanated from the international obligations Seychelles had under the *NPT* and the *Human Rights Charter.*

The laws pertaining to REI are meant for the advancement of the ordinary person and the development of states and a region, and in such circumstances where necessary sovereignty must be limited to ensure development and growth within a state or region, so as not to upset the common shared value system. Fagboyibo states:

> The corollary of establishing these organisations is the transfer of sovereignty or powers necessary for the fulfilment of tasks. While states continue to cling to sovereignty, there is also a realisation of the need to boost the functional abilities of these organisations. The divisibility of sovereignty becomes inevitable. [143]

The logic that gaverise to the judgment of the Seychelles SCA must also apply for the purposes of REI. States engaging in REI share a common interest, and when a member state acts in breach of the region's agreements it injures the regional community as a whole.

3.4 The SADC's approach to legal reception as an obstacle for REI

Article 6(4) of the *SADC Treaty* provides that "Member states shall take all steps necessary to ensure the uniform application of this treaty."[144]Uniformity of laws in all aspects would guarantee the realization of REI within the SADC region. However, the manner in which these laws are to be received into the municipal laws of the states as prescribed by the treaty itself leaves a lot to be desired.

---

142 United Nations International Law Report (2006) Fragmentation of International Law 193.

143 Fagboyibo 2011 *SAYIL* 211.

144 A 6(4) of the *SADC Treaty*.

Article 40 provides that "This treaty shall be ratified by the signatory states in accordance with their constitutional procedures."[145] Article 40 is rather dualistic in nature, a fact which has led to an unstable legal framework. The effect of subjecting SADC community laws to the constitutional provisions of member states is the creation of an unstable legal frame work. Saurombe says:[146]

> The SADC's economic integration process, and community state, interstate and inter-community legal relations are situated on an unstable legal frame work, and attempts to provide a legal framework have been incomplete and sometimes grounded on questionable assumptions.

The SADC as an institution does not itself embrace the supranational quality it possesses. The SADC must understand that the arena of law it has entered into by forming the REC is a "new legal order of international law" which operates differently from traditional international law.[147]The SADC has submitted itself to the municipal laws of states and has not embraced its uniqueness in pursuit of what it sought to achieve as provided in Article 5(1) (a), which reads:[148]

> Achieve development and economic growth, alleviate poverty, enhance the standard and quality of life of the peoples of Southern Africa and support the socially disadvantaged through regional integration.

Article 40 of the *SADC Treaty* has created an exit opportunity which member states can use to defer or not to fulfil their treaty obligations. The member states will uphold the supremacy of their constitutional provisions at the expense of the SADC law. But the *VCLT* provides under article 27 that "A party may not invoke the provisions of its internal law as justification for its failure to perform a treaty..." Article 40 of the *SADC Treaty* is a direct violation of article 27 of the *VCLT,* as it indirectly leaves room for member states to plead their municipal laws as a reason for not fulfilling their international obligations.

Most constitutional provisions have a supremacy clause, and even if the laws of a member state are contra to the *SADC Treaty* the constitutional provisions will prevail, simply

---

145 A 40 of the *SADC Treaty.*
146 Saurombe 2013 *LDD*.470.
147 See para 2.2.1 Is REI governed by international law?
148 A 5 of the *SADC Treaty.*

because the treaty itself will be received in the member states municipal laws as far as the constitutional provisions allow it to be received. Oppong agrees with this point of view:[149]

> The reliance on national constitutional measures to give effect to community law is one of the principle reasons for the failure of Africa's economic integration process, at least to the extent that the presence of the communities is not immediately felt at the national level.

Article 40 obstructs what the SADC seeks to achieve as provided in Article 5 (1) (a) of the *SADC Treaty*. It has created a lacuna in law and has paved the way for member states to hide behind the legislative procedures of their municipal laws as a way of avoiding their set obligations in treaty law, as will be evidenced by examining Zimbabwe's approach to REI.

3.4.1 Conflict between the SADC treaty and the Zimbabwean constitution

In the case of Mike *Campbell Pty Ltd v The Republic of Zimbabwe* [150](Campbell decision) the SADC tribunal had to determine the obligations of the Zimbabwean government as provided for under the SADC community laws. As the SADC had been formed by means of the *SADC Treaty,* the principles of international law had to apply.[151]

The applicant was a white Zimbabwean citizen who was challenging the land reform programme embarked upon by the Zimbabwean government. He had become a victim of this initiative when the Zimbabwean government seized his farm in the district of Chegutu. Seventy-nine other white farmers also joined the applicant in this matter. The applicants contended that the land reform programme was unlawful because it was a discriminatory exercise which targeted white Zimbabweans only, thereby violating article 6(2) of the *SADC Treaty.*[152] The applicants challenged the Zimbabwean government's actions and argued that those actions and the provisions of Amendment 17 of Zimbabwe's

---

149 Oppong "Making regional economic community laws enforceable in national legal systems-constitutional and judicial challenges." 154.

150 SADC (T) 2/2007.

151 SADC (T) 2/2007 par 15, p17.

152 A 6(2) *SADC Treaty* and member states shall not discriminate against any person on grounds of gender, religion, political views, race, ethnic origin, culture or disability.

constitution were a complete affront to the principles of the SADC treaty, which sought to uphold human rights, democracy and the rule of law.[153]

The Zimbabwean government did not perceive the land reform programme as unlawful because the programme was constitutionally recognised under section 16 A of the constitution.[154] The Zimbabwean legislature further entrenched this provision through the constitutions under Section 16B (amendment 17).[155] Moreover, the Constitution contained the supremacy clause, which was provided under section 3.[156]

The respondent further stated that the SADC tribunal did not have jurisdiction to hear the matter because Zimbabwe had not followed its legislative process to ensure that the Amendment on the Protocol of the Tribunal had been enacted and incorporated into Zimbabwe's municipal laws. Hence, Zimbabwe was not bound by the decisions of the SADC tribunal or any of its findings. His Excellency Justice Mondlane ruled:[157]

> It is clear to us that the tribunal has jurisdiction in respect of any dispute concerning human rights, democracy and the rule of law, which are the very issues raised in the present application. Moreover, the respondent cannot rely on its national law, namely, amendment to avoid its legal obligations under the treaty.[158]

It was on the basis of this averment that the SADC tribunal ruled in favour of the applicant to the following effect:

(a) Amendment 17 was a violation of the *SADC Treaty* and a breach of Article 4(c) and 6 (2) of the *SADC Treaty*.

(b) The government of Zimbabwe had to pay fair compensation to the three applicants who had already been evicted on a fixed date.

---

153 A 4(c) of the *SADC Treaty* reads: SADC and its member states shall act in accordance with the following principles, human rights, democracy and the rule of law.
154 Constitution of the Republic of Zimbabwe, 2000.
155 *Constitution of the Republic of Zimbabwe*, 2005.
156 Section Three of Zimbabwe's old constitution read: "This constitution is the supreme law of Zimbabwe and if any other law is inconsistent with this constitution that other law shall, to the extent of the inconsistency, be void."
157 Judgement delivered by H.E Justice Dr Luis Antonio Mondlane.
158 SADC (T) 2/2007 paras 28, 25.

(c) The government was directed to take all necessary measures to protect the possession, occupation and ownership of the lands of the applicants and to ensure that no action was taken, pursuant to Amendment 17, to evict the applicants from their lands or to interfere with their peaceful residence thereon.

3.4.1.1 The enforcement of the Campbell decision in the municipal law of Zimbabwe

In the matter *Gramara Private Ltd v Government of the Republic of Zimbabwe* (*Gramara decision*)[159]the court had to determine if the Campbell decision passed at the SADC tribunal was enforceable in Zimbabwe. To determine the issue of enforcing the decisions of the tribunal, Patel J resorted to the provisions of the *Protocol on the tribunal* (the *protocol*), which provided under article 32 that the laws and rules of civil procedure of the country which ought to enforce the tribunal decision would be followed.[160]The applicant argued that the decision of the SADC tribunal was binding on Zimbabwe and Zimbabwe could not use its municipal laws as a means to avoid its obligations under treaty law.[161]Acting in compliance with article 32 of the protocol Patel J stated:[162]

> The overall effect of these provisions is that the decisions of the tribunal are binding and enforceable within the territories of member states, which are under an obligation to take the measures necessary for the execution of these decisions. However, such enforcement is governed by the rules of civil procedure for the registration and enforcement of foreign judgements which are in force in the territory of the state in which the particular judgement is to be enforced. In other words, it is the domestic rules of procedure of each member state as opposed to any uniform adjectival law of the tribunal which must govern the enforcement of a given judgement in the territory of that state.[163]

Patel J resorted to the *Civil Matters Mutual Assistance Act* [164] of the Zimbabwean law, which provided that in enforcing foreign judgements common law had to be used. Since

---

159 HC 33/09 Zimbabwe High Court 2010.

160 A 32 of the protocol reads: The law and rules of civil procedure for the registration and enforcement of foreign judgements in force in the territory of the state in which the judgement is to be enforced shall govern enforcement.

161 A 32(3) reads: Decisions of the tribunal shall be binding upon the parties to the dispute in respect of that particular case and enforceable within the territories of the states concerned; The rule of *pacta sunt servanda.*

162 HC 33/09 Zimbabwe High Court 2010.

163 HC 33/09 Zimbabwe High Court 2010 at para 11 4.

164 Chapter 8:02.

there was no authority within Zimbabwe pertaining to enforcing foreign judgements, Patel J borrowed the standards set in South Africa, another common law country. Patel J resorted to the requirements set in *Jones v Krok*.[165] However, for the purposes of this case the following requirements were in dispute:

(i) Did the SADC tribunal have international jurisdictional competence?

(ii) Would enforcing the SADC tribunal decision not be contrary to public policy?

3.4.1.2 Did the SADC tribunal have international jurisdiction competence?

The Zimbabwean government in this regard stated that the agreement on amending the protocol had never been ratified by Zimbabwe or by the prescribed number of SADC member states as provided for in the main treaty under article 22.[166] As far as Zimbabwe was concerned, the tribunal lacked jurisdiction and the Campbell decision could not be enforced in Zimbabwe.

However, Patel J was able to clearly set out the relation between the SADC tribunal and Zimbabwean courts. Reference was made to the *VCLT*, which provides that when a state is considered to be bound by a treaty it expresses its consent by signing, ratification, and acceptance, or by other means if so agreed.[167] Reflecting on how consent to be bound was provided for in the *SADC Treaty*, Patel J made it clear that the manner in which the *SADC Treaty* would be ratified and when it would enter into force were provided for under articles 39 and 41 of the *SADC Treaty*,[168]but how an amendment to a protocol would enter into force was a different issue. The *SADC Treaty* provided that an amendment to

---

165 1995(1) SA 677(A).
i. The foreign court that gave judgement must have international jurisdiction or competence.
ii. The judgement given was final and conclusive in effect
iii. Recognition and enforcement of the judgement would not be contrary to public policy.
iv. The judgement was not obtained by fraudulent means.
v. The judgement does not involve the enforcement of a penal or revenue law of a foreign state.
vi. Enforcement of the judgement is not precluded by the provisions of the Protection of Business Act 99 of 1978 as amended.

166 A 22 of the *SADC Treaty* reads: "Each protocol shall be subject to signature and ratification by the parties."

167 A 40 of the *VCLT*.

168 A 39 reads: "This treaty shall be signed by the high contracting parties." Article 41 reads: "This treaty shall enter into force thirty days after the deposit of the instruments of ratification by two thirds of the states listed in the preamble".

a treaty should be adopted by three quarters of all the member states of the Community.[169] In this regard Patel J stated:[170]

> To conclude this aspect of the case my assessment of and determination of the jurisdictional capacity of the tribunal is as follows: On the 14th of August 2001, the amendment agreement was signed by 13 out of 14 heads of state, including Zimbabwe, thereby concluding the process of its adoption and entry into force. In my view there can be no doubt whatsoever that the agreement was duly adopted in terms of article 36(1) of the treaty and that it became binding upon all the member states on the date of its adoption.[171]

For the purposes of the amendment of the protocol on the tribunal, Patel considered the amendments to be directly applicable as provided for under article 36 of the *SADC treaty*, so there was no need for ratification or for the legislative procedures of member states to determine if the *Protocol on the Tribunal* would apply in its municipal laws. Patel J stated:

> It also follows that the republic of Zimbabwe thereupon became subject to the jurisdiction of the tribunal and that the jurisdictional competence of the tribunal in the Campbell case which was determined in 2008 cannot be disputed. The respondent's position in this regard, [premised on the ex post facto official pronouncements repudiating the tribunal's jurisdiction], is essentially erroneous and misconceived. Their position is rendered even more untenable by the conduct of SADC governments, including the government of Zimbabwe, subsequent to the adoption of the Amendment agreement, which conduct has been entirely consistent with the provisions of the treaty as amended by agreement.[172]

It stems from this reasoning that Patel found that the SADC tribunal had jurisdictional competence in the *Campbell case* and hence one of the requirements of enforcing the Campbell decision within Zimbabwe had been fully met.

3.4.1.3. Enforcing the Campbell decision v Public Policy

In evaluating whether or not enforcing the *Campbell case* decision would be contra to public policy, Patel J stated that public policy varies depending on the circumstances and values within a society. Patel asked two questions pertaining to public policy, which were:

---

169 A 36 *SADC Treaty*, A 10 of the *SADC Treaty*.
170 HC 33/09 Zimbabwe High Court 2010.
171 HC 33/09 Zimbabwe High Court 2010 para 42 12.
172 HC 33/09 Zimbabwe High Court 2010 para 42 12.

(a) Was it consistent with the public policy of Zimbabwe not to recognise and enforce the decision of the tribunal at the municipal level?

(b) Was it in the interest of the public policy of Zimbabwe for the SADC tribunal's judgement to impugn the legality of the land reform programme sanctioned by the supreme court of Zimbabwe?

With regards to the first enquiry Patel J correctly found that it was contrary to Zimbabwe's public policy not to enforce the SADC tribunal's decision, because Zimbabwe was bound by international custom as well as by the SADC tribunal to uphold such decisions. He went on to state that by virtue of the fact that Zimbabwe was bound by the Protocol on the tribunal and the *SADC Treaty*, Zimbabwe had created an enforceable legitimate expectation both within and beyond the borders of Zimbabwe that it would comply.

Patel J stated that it was not in the interest of the public policy of Zimbabwe for the SADC tribunal's judgement to impugn the legality of the land reform programme sanctioned by the supreme court of Zimbabwe.[173] Patel J used the constitution as a means by which Zimbabwe could evade its obligations under the SADC laws. He stated:[174]

> As already indicated, the applicants' land was acquired by the government in terms of section 16B of the constitution without any compensation payable in respect of the land itself. If the tribunal's judgement were to be registered by this court and subsequently voluntarily complied with or enforced by court orders, the government would be required to contravene and disregard what parliament has specifically enacted in section 16B of the Constitution.[175]

The rationale behind his finding was that the laws of Zimbabwe can never be subordinate to the laws of any other regimes, as the Zimbabwean constitution had a supremacy clause.[176] He provided that in as much as the common law finds it plausible to enforce

173 Advancing national interests at the expense of international interests is the ultimate result of following the dualist theory. Cassese considers this as an emergency exit for member states where they feel their national interests are threatened.

174 HC 33/09 Zimbabwe High Court 2010.

175 HC 33/09 Zimbabwe High Court 2010.par 48, 18.

176 Section 3 of the Zimbabwean Constitution.

the SADC tribunal's judgement, common law must be applied to conform to the constitution.[177] He stated:[178]

> I consider it to be patently contrary to the public policy of any country, including Zimbabwe, to require its government to act in a manner that is manifestly incompatible with what is constitutionally ordained.

It is rather unfortunate that Patel J found his judgement by this means.[179] Patel J failed to consider the nature of the institution which had reached the decision he ought to have enforced. He did not consider the fact that the SADC was a supranational entity and that its laws were supreme.

Patel J rejects the application that the Campbell decision be enforced in Zimbabwe on the basis of the public policy exception, because he equates enforcing the SADC tribunal's judgement in a member states' municipal laws to enforcing a foreign a judgement, as prescribed by the SADC treaty under article 32(1) of the Protocol on the Tribunal. On this issue De Wet states:[180]

> It is unusual for the treaties regulating the competencies of international tribunals to determine that their decisions shall be treated as foreign judgements on the domestic level. Instead international decisions are usually to be treated as domestic judgements. A crucial difference is the fact that the recognition and enforcement of a foreign judgement can be denied where it would result in a violation of public policy. The public policy exception is well established in the conflicts of law context, including where the enforcement of other national jurisdictions is at stake. However, it does not fit in a regime based on public international law such as the SADC regime, where states can use their domestic law as an excuse for not implementing their international obligations.

Equating the SADC tribunal's decisions to foreign judgements strips the SADC of its international character. Article 32(1) of the SADC tribunal protocol weakens the institution, which must bow to issues of public policy in each of its member states separately. The tribunal's judgments were therefore not of a binding nature.[181]For an

---

177 Patel J "The notion of public policy cannot be deployed and insinuated under cover of the common law to circumvent or subvert the fundamental law of the land."
178 HC 33/09 Zimbabwe High Court 2010.
179 Patel emphasised the supremacy of the Zimbabwean constitution and also hinted that it was not in the public interest to compensate the seventy-nine applicants or for the government to reverse the land reform programme.
180 De Wet *The Rise and Fall of the SADC Tribunal.*
181 De Wet 2013 ICSID review11.

effective REC to function the institution must be able to assert itself and impose itself on its members.[182] The ECJ in the *San Michele Case* agrees:[183]

> Resort to rules or legal concepts of national law for appraisal of the validity of facts of community institutions would have the effect of impairing the unity and efficacy of community law. The validity of such acts can be appraised only in relation to community law. The law based on the treaty, an autonomous source of law, cannot by its nature be opposed by rules of national law of whatever kind without losing its character as community law and without the legal basis of the community itself being jeopardized; hence reliance on the impairment either of basic rights as formulated by the constitution of a member state or of the principles of a national constitutional structure cannot affect the validity of an act of the community or its effect within the territory of that state.

On the other hand, it would have been in line with public policy to ensure that the Campbell decision was enforced within Zimbabwe, as it would have given effect to its international obligations under international law, in accord with a legitimate expectation amongst its own people. In the matter *Minister of State for Immigration and Ethnic affairs v A Hin Teoh*[184]it was noted that the Australian government had signed the *United Nations Convention of the Rights of the Child*. The court ruled that although the convention had not been incorporated into Australian law it provided a legitimate expectation which parents and children could rely on.[185]Toohey J stated:[186]

> ...A submission by a decision maker that no regard at all need to be paid to Australia's acceptance of an international obligation by virtue of the ratification of a convention is unattractive. What is the next step? Ratification of itself does not make the obligations enforceable in the courts. Legislation, not executive act, is required. But the assumption of such an obligation may give rise to legitimate expectation in the minds of those who are affected by administrative decisions on which the obligation has some bearing.[187]

---

182 According to this view, there is no true supranationality unless the power of the group can not only assert itself in legal forms but also impose itself successfully on recalculating states.

183 22 June 1965 Case 9/65.

184 (1995) 183 CLR.

185 (1995) 183 CLR The minister disagreed with this, and Lee J stated: "But the fact that the convention has not been incorporated into Australian law does not mean that its ratification holds no significance for Australian law."

186 (1995) 183 CLR.

187 1995) 183 CLR par 29, 16; Barrie 1997 *S. African L.J* "The provisions of an international treaty to which the country is a party do not form part of municipal law unless those provisions have been validly incorporated into the country's municipal law by statute. This principle has as its foundation the proposition that the making and ratification of treaties fall within the province whereas the making and alteration of the law fall within the province of the legislature (parliament). Consequently, a treaty which has not been incorporated into Australian municipal law cannot operate as a direct source of

The courts have since maintained that not giving the force of effect to international obligations sends the wrong message that making such a commitment could amount to window dressing.[188] In passing his judgement Patel J also stated that states create an enforceable legitimate expectation for their citizens to use when they consent to be bound by treaties. Defining public policy through the lens of legitimate expectation would have made of it a justifiable reason for the enforcement of the *Campbell decision.*

3.5 COMESA's approach to legal reception and its effect on REI

COMESA has prescribed two ways in which its member states are to receive its laws into their municipal laws. Article 5 reads:

> (a) The member states shall make every effort to plan and direct their development policies with a view to creating conditions favourable for the achievement of the aims of the common market and the implementation of the provisions of this treaty and shall abstain from any measure likely to jeopardize the achievement of the aims of the common market or the implementation of this treaty.
> (b) Each member state shall take steps to secure the enactment of and the continuation of such legislation to give effect to this treaty and in particular
> (i) To confer upon the common market legal capacity and personality required for the performance of its functions and
> (ii) To confer upon the regulations of the council the force of law and the necessary legal effect within its territory.[189]

Whereas article 12(1) states:

> Regulations shall be published in the official Gazette of the Common Market and shall enter into force on the date of their publication or such later date as may be specified in the regulations.

The two provisions are different in their approach to how COMESA community law will be received into the member states' municipal laws. Article 5 seems to provide that member states must ensure that the common market laws are incorporated by legislative means,

---

individual rights or individual obligations under Australian law." 475 Mason CJ and Deane CJ, however, maintained a dualist approach.

188 *Tavita v Minister of Immigration* [1994] 2NZLR 257.

189 A 5 of the *COMESA Treaty*

whereas article 12 can be interpreted to mean that the laws will have force and effect once published. In other words, the regulations do not need to be adopted by member states and enacted by legislative means but are directly applicable.

3.5.1 The Polytol Paints case: An exposé of the COMESA legal frame work

The COMESA Court of Justice in the landmark case of *Polytol Paints & Adhesive Manufacturers Co. Ltd v The Republic of Mauritius*[190] (Polytol Paints case) shed some light on the manner in which the *COMESA Treaty* would be interpreted.

The applicant in this case was a company duly registered in terms of Mauritian law. In 1993 Mauritius became a member of the COMESA and signed the *COMESA Treaty,* which was incorporated into its municipal laws as a schedule to Mauritius' Customs Act. The treaty provided under article 46 that member states had to ensure that all customs duties would be eliminated by the year 2000 for common market treatment.[191] Mauritius did indeed ensure that by year 2000 all customs duties pertaining to the COMESA manufactured goods were duty free.

However, on 16 November 2001 the Mauritian government went on to introduce 40% customs duty on specific products imported from Egypt, following a bilateral agreement which the two member states had entered into. This action was a complete violation of the *COMESA Treaty.*

3.5.2 The effect of inconsistent application of an REC's laws in the light of the Polytol Paints Case

Now in the hope of establishing a zero rate duty amongst COMESA member states, Mauritius' actions in re-introducing the customs duty was retrogressive to the purpose and objectives sought by the COMESA. The Mauritian Government argued that the member states had the flexibility to determine when they could implement certain aspects of the treaty and that the requirement to eliminate duties by 2000 as provided in Article 46 was "not cast in stone".

---

190 Case No 1 of 2012.
191 A 46 of the *COMESA Treaty.*

The Mauritian government's argument stems from the fact that article 5 waits upon the member states to give the treaty the recognition it requires in municipal law, whereas the treaty can apply directly in the member states' municipal laws to ensure uniformity and certainty. The negative effect of subjecting REI laws to the constitutional provisions of member states is that the member states give a different interpretation to the treaty provisions and in most cases they give an interpretation that best suits them. In this instance the flexible approach argument advanced by the Mauritian government was meant to suit their own position.

3.5.3 When municipal laws override the COMESA Treaty

The applicant had earlier brought its case before the municipal courts, which upheld municipal laws over the *COMESA Treaty*.[192]When the applicant approached the *Supreme Court of Appeal* (hereinafter referred to as SCA) of Mauritius, the court stated:[193]

> This court can only consider the validity of the regulations against the backdrop of the Customs Tariff Act and our Constitution. In the absence of any such legislation to that effect, non-fulfilment by Mauritius of its obligations, if any under the COMESA Treaty, is not enforceable by national courts.

Unfortunately, the *Customs Tariff Act*[194] which annexed the *COMESA Treaty* was repealed and replaced by the *Mauritius Customs Tariff Regulation of 2001*.[195] In this regard the SCA of Mauritius used its municipal law as a justification for its failure to fulfil its treaty obligations, which is contra to the *VCLT*, which provides under article 27 that "A party may not invoke the provisions of its internal law as justification for its failure to perform a treaty." This is also the case with Zimbabwe, as described earlier.

---

192 A 26 of the *COMESA Treaty*.

193 *Polytol Paints and Adhesive Manufacturers Co Ltd v The Minister of Finance* 2009 SCJ 106.

194 59 of 1969.

195 Under act 15 of 2006.

3.5.4 Non-fulfilment of treaty obligations and accountability in COMESA

The applicant further required the COMESA Court of Justice to make a determination pertaining to the non-fulfilment of treaty obligations. The applicant considered non-fulfilment in the following manner:

(a) Failing to take steps to implement or properly implement the Treaty within its domestic legislation;

(b) Failing to give the treaty the force of law and the necessary legal effect within its territory; and

(c) Failing to give its national courts jurisdiction to deal with matters concerning the application and interpretation of the treaty.

Pertaining to the non-fulfilment of treaty obligations within the COMESA, the court stated that the applicant could not plead these matters. Lord Principle Rugege went on to provide that when it comes to the non-fulfilment of treaty obligations, the responsibility is on member states and the secretary general to make such an argument, and not on an individual citizen.[196]

Lord Principle Rugege relied on article 24, which reads:[197]

> A member state which considers that another member state or the Council has failed to fulfil an obligation under this treaty or has infringed a provision of this treaty may refer the matter to the court.

Lord Principle Rugege went on to cite article 26, which provides:[198]

> Any person who is resident in a Member state may refer for determination by the court the legality of any act, regulation, directive or decision of the council or of a member state on the grounds that such Act, directive, decision or regulation is unlawful or an infringement of the provisions of this treaty.

---

196 Thus a legal or natural person is permitted to bring to Court only matters relating to conduct or measures that are unlawful or an infringement of the treaty, but not the non-fulfilment of Treaty obligations by a member state.

197 A 24 of the *COMESA Treaty*.

198 A 26 of the *COMESA Treaty*.

In the *Polytol Paints Case* non-fulfilment of the treaty occurred by means of passing a regulation that made it impossible for article 46 of the *COMESA Treaty* to be fulfilled. The Customs Tariff Regulation of 2000 introduced a 40% customs duty on specific products contra to article 46.[199]

But Lord Principle Rugege gave a narrow interpretation of who can invoke non-fulfilment of a treaty obligation, left the issue open to member states alone, and decided that article 26 of the *COMESA Treaty* did not afford natural or juristic persons such privilege. Although it is not explicitly stated under article 26 that a natural or juristic person can bring a member state to task for non-fulfilment, the provision impliedly suggests so.

Lord Principle Rugege's interpretation pertaining to the non-fulfilment of treaty obligations is not helpful to the achievement o of REI, especially in Africa, where one cannot expect member states to take each other to task for the non-fulfilment of treaty obligations. The principle of solidarity which permeates within African RECs may be the cause of this. [200]

> Unlike the interpretation of solidarity in the 1960s which meant emancipation of all Africans, the behaviour of the SADC member states demonstrates an alternative interpretation of solidarity to mean standing together in support of the actions of member state governments, even if doing so violates the emancipation project.

This is also true for COMESA member states, where in this instance two member states of the same regional grouping act together in defying the objectives and plans of the RECs they belong to. In instances where the issue of non-fulfilment is not pursued by other member states, there is a need to turn to natural or juristic persons to ensure that member states fulfil their obligations, as is expected of them. Excluding natural or juristic persons from this process would be unproductive.

It would have been much more desirable if Lord Principle Rugege had stretched the net of accountability wide enough to accommodate natural or juristic persons, so that in instances where member states act in cohesion to violate treaty provisions, individuals can also raise a red flag to that effect before the court of justice. It is highly unlikely that

---

199 A 46 of the *COMESA Treaty*.
200 Anon *Rethinking and theorizing regional integration in Southern Africa* .133.

a third member state will claim non-fulfilment of treaty obligations in issues where it does not have direct interest, but individuals who are directly affected would be more motivated in that regard. Fobayibo states:[201]

> Another method of ensuring compliance is the involvement of the civil society in transnational policy making process. Not only will this enhance the legitimacy of regional institutions, it also ensures a keen sense of ownership by the people. This kind of participation ensures that citizens will become more cognisant of the origins of rules and regulations, the obligations of member states and the compliance mechanisms. In addition, enhanced participation will propel civil society to get more involved in playing an indirect role in monitoring compliance, reporting infringements and exerting pressure on member states to comply.

The law must not give the opportunity for redress to member states alone but also to civil society and individual citizens who are directly affected by such decisions. However, Lord Principle Rugege was able to disqualify Mauritius' argument where it submitted it had entered into a bilateral agreement with Egypt in which they agreed to increase import duties despite that agreement being contra to the main treaty.[202]This act was done in the name of solidarity, regardless of the effect it would have on the realization of REI in the COMESA. Lord Principal Rugege clearly stated that the bilateral act was clearly against the basic objectives of the *COMESA Treaty,* and referred to article 41 of the *VCLT,* which reads:

> Two or more parties to a multi-lateral treaty may conclude an agreement to modify the Treaty as between themselves alone if (i) the modification in question is not prohibited by the treaty and (ii) does not relate to a provision, derogation from which is incompatible with the effective execution of the object and purpose of the Treaty as a whole".[203]

201 Fagbayibo *CILSA* 2012 XLV.

202 A 56(3) of the *COMESA Treaty* provides that '"Nothing in this Treaty shall prevent two member states from entering into new preferential agreements among themselves which aim at achieving the objectives of the Common Market, provided that any preferential treatment accorded under such agreements is extended to the other Member States on a reciprocal and non-discriminatory basis."

203 A 41of the *VCLT.*

In this instance the Mauritius and Egypt bilateral agreement was a direct violation of article 46[204] and article 55[205] of the *COMESA Treaty*. Moreover, the *VCLT* provides in article 18 that parties to a treaty must refrain from acting contra to the treaty itself.[206]

When one assesses the principles of international law, it is clear that such an argument is not plausible in legal terms, because the *COMESA Treaty* is based on a shared value system in which the obligations are *erga omnes.* Every COMESA member state has an interest in the establishment of the Free Trade Area, and breaching the obligation to cooperate to that end runs counter to the value which is shared amongst the member states.

3.6 Southern Africa's REC judiciary as the driving force to the realisation of REI

The role of the ECJ in ensuring legal and economic certainty within the EEC has been fully expounded earlier on in this study[207]. Unfortunately, the situation in Southern Africa's RECs judicial arm vary in the manner in which they exert authority over their member states. There is a great disparity between the manner in which the judicial arms of the SADC and the COMESA function. The SADC created various institutions, one of them being the SADC tribunal, although the tribunal has been suspended indefinitely.[208] However, when one closely examines the SADC treaty as a whole one notes that the SADC tribunal is not totally independent. Ruppel and Bangamwabo have defined judicial independence as:[209]

> The degree to which judges believe they can decide and do decide consistent with their own personal attitudes, values and conceptions of judicial role(in the interpretation of the law), in opposition to what others, who have or are believed to have political or judicial power, think about or desire in like matters, and particularly

---

204 A 46 *COMESA Treaty.*

205 A 55 of the *COMESA Treaty.*

206 A 18 of the *VCLT*.

207 See para 2.4.2.1.

208 See Erasmus *The new protocol for the SADC Tribunal: Jurisdictional changes and implication of SADC.* Article 9(f) of the *SADC Treaty* reads: The following institutions are hereby established: the tribunal. Article 16 (1) further states: The tribunal shall be constituted to ensure adherence to and the proper interpretation of the provisions of this treaty and subsidiary instruments and to adjudicate upon such disputes as may be referred to it.

209 Becker in Ruppel and Bangamwabo *The SADC Tribunal*: 179.

> when a decision adverse to the beliefs or desires of those with political or judicial power may bring some retribution on the judges personally or on the power of the court.

The summit is considered the supreme policy maker of the SADC and it has the powers to give orders to all other sub-ordinate institutions, which include the tribunal itself. Article 10 of the *SADC Treaty* provides: [210]

> (1) The summit shall consist of the heads of state or Government of all member states and shall be the supreme policy making institution. (2) The summit shall be responsible for the overall policy direction and control of the functions of SADC. (3) The summit shall adapt legal instruments for the implementation of the provisions of this treaty; provided that the summit may delegate this authority to the council or any other institutions of SADC as the SADC may deem appropriate. Unless otherwise provided in this treaty, the decisions of the summit shall be consensus and binding.

Saurombe states: [211]

> ...the European Council is an embodiment of controlled power while the SADC summit is an institution with too much power. This clearly will not work for regional integration in the SADC. There has to be a measure of control in the SADC as is exercised in the EU.

Fagboyibo also expresses an opinion: [212]

> A major impediment to operationalising supranationalism in Africa is the fact that regional institutions are not independent enough to implement integration initiatives. These institutions are expected to operate in accordance with the whim of member states... There is a strong nexus between the effective implementation of integration initiatives and the autonomy of regional institutions. The ability of these institutions to act where member states in respect of specific of common interest ensures that integration is firmly placed in capable and neutral hands and insulated from the vagaries of national politics.

With such a framework, when the SADC tribunal attempts to bridge the gap that is created by the member states' different approaches to legal reception by ensuring that all legal provisions are uniformly applied, there is the possibility that the summit will trump such decisions, which will inevitably slow down the REI process.

---

210 A 10 of the *SADC Treaty*.

211 Saurombe 2013 *LDD* 245.

212 Fagboyibo 2013 *PER* .19.

The SADC tribunal also does not have the powers to issue remedies for non-compliance. De Wet rightly states:[213]

> The tribunal itself does not have the competence to order remedies for non-compliance and reporting such a finding to the summit. It is then up to the summit, in accordance with Article 33(1) and 33(2), to impose sanctions on a country which persistently fails without good reason to fulfil obligations assumed under the SADC treaty.

The powers of the summit in this instance weaken the effective functioning of the judiciary, because the decisions that are made in an attempt to bring the laws in uniformity eventually become useless as these decisions tend not to be enforced, or the summit may choose to sit on the tribunal's findings in an attempt at political appeasement. There is no political will amongst the heads of states who form the summit to single out another member state for non-compliance. Instead, member states prefer to turn a blind eye to the treaty violations of fellow member states.

However, with COMESA the situation is rather different. The Court of Justice was established as one of the institutions of the community, but it is independent of any other organ, even of the highest the authority.[214]The COMESA Court of Justice can therefore ensure uniform application of the law and policies emanating from the *COMESA Treaty* without being second guessed by a higher authority and this may ultimately lead to the attainment of REI. The *COMESA Treaty* has in itself provided under article 29 that "Decisions of the court on the interpretation of the provisions of this treaty shall have precedence over decisions of national courts".[215]

The *New Protocol on the Tribunal in SADC* has now limited the jurisdiction of the tribunal. The statement that the tribunal will have "material jurisdiction" implies that it will have jurisdiction over the parties to the protocol and not over all member states of the

---

213 De Wet 2013 *ICSID review* 14.

214 A 8 of the *COMESA Treaty* provides: "The direction and decisions of the Authority taken or given in pursuance of the provisions of this treaty, shall as the case maybe, be binding on the member states and on all organs of the common market other than the court in the exercise of its jurisdiction and on those to whom they may be addressed under this treaty".

215 A 29 of the *COMESA Treaty*.

SADC.[216]What is more disturbing is the fact that in the new protocol member states have the opportunity to opt out, in which case they will not be bound by the tribunal or any of its decisions.[217] Article 50 of the new protocol provides:

> (a) A state party may withdraw from this protocol upon the expiration of twelve (12) months from the date of giving written notice to that effect to the executive secretary.
> (b) Such state party shall cease to enjoy all rights and benefits under this protocol upon the withdrawal becoming effective.
> (c) Notwithstanding the provisions of paragraphs 1&2, such state party shall continue to be bound by obligations that arise out of this protocol and are outstanding on the date of the withdrawal until such obligations are discharged.

What this provision does is to give member states the leeway not to be bound by the provisions or any decisions which the tribunal would have made, which is a loophole making for inconsistencies. It also denies the opportunity to other member states to hold the opting out state accountable if it violates any other provisions after it has opted out. The arm of the law cannot touch the opting out party again. This is a recipe for inconsistency and uncertainty, which makes the achievement of REI a daunting task.

Erasmus[218]argues that the protocol on the tribunal is an integral part of the *SADC Treaty* and hence that member states cannot opt out. He further states that the wording of the above provision has confused the fundamental principle, which was that the tribunal had jurisdiction over all member states.[219]This signals the death of the judicial arm in the SADC region, as such a move will guarantee inconsistency and uncertainty about how the treaty will apply.[220]

Pertaining to jurisdiction, COMESA is a different ball game altogether. It has maintained compulsory jurisdiction over all parties and there is no protocol relating to the court of

216 A 33 of the New Protocol on the Tribunal.

217 A 50 of the New Protocol. on the Tribunal

218 Erasmus The new protocol for the SADC Tribunal.

219 Erasmus *The new protocol for the SADC Tribunal.* "The tribunal exercises its jurisdiction over all member states but the wording of the new protocol casts doubt on this fundamental principle. Withdrawal should not be possible, the protocol is an integral part of the treaty. Article 16 of the treaty has not been amended and remains in force."12.

220 Erasmus *The new protocol for the SADC Tribunal* notes that the treaty has stated itself that the protocol on the Tribunal is expressly part of the treaty as provided in article 16, a statement which is confirmed by Article 2 of the new protocol.

justice.[221] The duties and all matters pertaining to the COMESA Court of Justice are included in the *COMESA Treaty.*

3.7 Conclusion

Although the law was considered as a strategy to realise REI in the case of the SADC under the RISDP and in the case of the COMESA under the MTSP, on careful consideration it becomes evident that there are many factors that contribute to weakening the effectiveness of using the law as a strategy. The effectiveness of the law as a strategy depends wholly on the manner in which a REC deermines how its own laws will be received within the municipal laws of the member states. Most Southern African states follow the dualist theory when incorporating international law within their own municipal laws. An exposé of why the dualist approach impacts negatively upon the realisation of REI has been made.

Unfortunately, the two RECs require member states to incorporate the REI laws within their municipal laws according to their own constitutional provisions, which makes attaining legal certainty difficult to attain. This is one of the main reasons why the attempt to realise a REI is making no progress in the region. It is good to be able to note, though, that the COMESA Court of Justice has been able to affirm its supremacy, as evidenced by the discussion in this chapter.

The judicial arms of the two RECs in Southern Africa are entirely different. That in the SADC has been weakened, whereas that in COMESA it is still authoritative and independent. The disparities go to show which of the two RECs is more likely to be able to ensure the laws are uniformly applied as a means to attain REI.

221 A 23(1) of the *COMESA Treaty* provides: "The court shall have jurisdiction to adjudicate upon all matters which may be referred to it pursuant to this treaty."

Chapter 4: Regional mandates and national approaches - a focus on South African constitutional provisions

4.1 Introduction

It has been established that legal integration has been considered by the SADC as a strategy that will lead to the realisation of REI in Southern Africa. In order to provide a practical example of how this process takes place, focus will be directed on one of the member states in the SADC to assess if and to what extent using the law as a strategy to ensure REI is being adopted within its own territory.

The country to consider at this point is South Africa, which has been described as the economic powerhouse of the SADC.[222] South Africa is thought to be one of the most advanced countries in Africa. It has a strong financial system and exports large volumes of raw materials and value-added goods.[223] According to the World Bank's ranking of economies, South Africa is the country with the most viable economy in the SADC region.[224] 55.5 % of the SADC's Gross Domestic Product (GDP) emanates from South Africa.[225] It is estimated that 58.7% of all imports into and 46.2% of all exports out of SADC member states are destined for or originate from South Africa.[226] Because of South Africa's economic muscle, REI is in its interest.

It is from this context that this chapter will assess legal reception in South Africa to determine if the manner in which South Africa implements international agreements impacts upon the realisation of REI in Southern Africa. An analysis of South Africa's constitutional provisions will be made, and reference will be made to South Africa's case law.

---

222 Lee 2011 http://www.osisa.org.
223 SADC country profile 2012 http://www.sadc.int/member-states/South-Africa.
224 World Bank rankings 2014 http:www.//doingbusiness.org.
225 African Development Bank (AFDB) 2015 http://www.africaneconomicoutlook.org.
226 (AFDB) 2015 http://www.africaneconomicoutlook.org.

4.2 Historical influences on South Africa's legal reception of international law

South Africa is a common law and civil law country, which means that it has a hybrid legal system.[227]The country's legal system comprises of the legal systems that were in the parent jurisdictions of its colonisers.[228] When the Dutch settled in the cape, Roman Dutch law became the predominant legal system. Because the Roman Dutch law subscribes to the monist approach, when Roman Dutch law was applied in South Africa international law would apply directly in the municipal laws of the state.[229]This has been considered to be the main reason why customary international law applies directly in South Africa's municipal law, as was highlighted in the case of *Nduli v Minister of Justice.*[230]

Turning to the flip side of the coin, when the British took occupation of the Cape English law became dominant at the Cape and spread through the whole of South Africa.[231] Britain's being a dualist country led to South Africa's evolving into a dualist state with regard to international agreements.[232] For international agreements to have the force and effect of law within the municipal laws of South Africa, there is a need for such agreements to be enacted by parliament.[233]

It is in terms of the continuing outcomes of the two major influences, Roman Dutch and English law, that one can understand the manner in which international law is received

---

227 Van Der Merwe *Fundamina* 18(1) 2012.

228 See para 3.3.

229 Dugard *International Law: A South African Perspective* 43.

230 1978 (1) SA 893(A).

231 Van Der Merwe *Fundamina*18(1) 2012. "The somewhat more sophisticated English constitutional law settled conflicts between the Dutch settlers and English rulers. Once the principles of English constitutional and administrative law had been adopted in the Cape, the Dutch principles of public law were completely eclipsed".

232 Sloss *et al* 476-503 "When it comes to treaties, the United Kingdom is very much a dualist state. A proper understanding of how treaties are implemented and enforced in the English legal system requires a reasonably detailed description of this form of dualism. It is also important because most of the other fifty-two commonwealth states are former British overseas territories that inherited the same, or very similar, constitutional principles about the place of treaties in domestic laws." 476.

233 See para 2.3.2.

in South Africa. The hybrid nature of South Africa's legal system his described by Scholtz and Ferreirra as follows:[234]

> Some states such as South Africa do not follow an exclusive monist or an exclusive dualist approach. For example, with regard to customary international law, section 232 of the constitution of the Republic of South Africa 1996 provides that it forms part of South African law as it is not in conflict with the constitution or an act of parliament. Pertaining to treaty law, section 231 determines that a treaty has to be transformed by way of an act of parliament in order to bring it within the ambit of South African law. The South African approach towards the relationship between international law and South African law can consequently be described as a hybrid in so far as a monist approach is followed with regard to customary international law and a dualist approach pertaining to treaty law.

Pre 1994, South Africa was a country that operated in isolation because of its apartheid policies. The apartheid policies were contra to the tenor of international human rights law which the international community had wholly embraced. South Africa is described as having been a "pariah" within the international community.[235] Post 1994, with the coming of the new constitution, South Africa was now dubbed as an "international law friendly country".[236]South Africa was quick to join the SADC in 1994, tapping into the REI agenda.[237]

International law has been firmly asserted within South Africa's Constitution.[238]The constitutional court (hereinafter referred to as CC) in *Glenister v The President of the Republic of South Africa* [239](hereinafter referred to as the *Glenister Case*)[240] affirmed the

---

234 Scholtz and Ferreirra *Zao RV* 71 (2011) 348.

235 Dugard *EJIL* 1.

236 Erasmus *SAYIL* 157; Sloss *et al The role of domestic courts in treaty enforcement; a comparative study.* 448-475 "The situation has changed dramatically since 1994.South Africa is today an active member of the international community and is a party to many multilateral and bilateral treaties. The South African constitution of 1996, an instrument that seeks to remedy the defects of its apartheid predecessors, is positively international law friendly".

237 Department of international relations and cooperation http://www.dfa.gov.za It is important to note that South Africa is also a member of the South African Customs Union (SACU), which is considered one of the oldest customs unions in the world. However, for the purposes of this research the focus will be placed on the SADC, which is the dominant REC in Southern Africa and which South Africa is a party to.

238 Constitution of the Republic of South Africa, 1996.

239 2011 (3) SA 347 (CC).

240 See para 4.3.1 for a detailed analysis of the case.

place of international law within South Africa's municipal laws. The majority judgement stated:[241]

> The constitution contains four provisions that regulate the impact of international law on the republic. One concerns the impact of international law on the interpretation of the bill of rights. A second concerns the status of international agreements. A third concerns customary international law. The constitution provides that it 'is law in the Republic unless it is inconsistent with the constitution or an Act of Parliament'. A fourth concerns the application of international law. It provides that when interpreting any legislation, 'every court must prefer any reasonable interpretation of the legislation that is consistent with international law over any alternative interpretation that is inconsistent with international law.'

It is important to understand the place of international law within the South African legal system because REI agreements are governed by international law, and knowing South Africa's position on international law will help determine the place of REI agreements within South African law. Having ascertained that South Africa tip-toes between the monist and dualist approach when receiving international law, it is important to examine the context and manner in which the two theories are applied within South Africa's constitutional provisions.

4.2.1 The monist approach to legal reception in South Africa

The monist theory applies within the *Constitution of the Republic of South Africa,* 1996(hereinafter referred to as the Constitution) when it pertains to customary international law. Section 232 of the constitution provides for the direct applicability of customary international law.[242]The status afforded to customary international law within the constitution is similar to the position prior to1994.Diemont J[243]in *South Atlantic Islands Development Corporation Ltd v Buchanan* stated:[244]

> Although I am surprised that there is no decision in which a South African Court has expressly asserted that international law forms part of our law, I would be even more surprised if there were a decision asserting the contrary. It appears to have been accepted in both the English and the American courts that international law forms

---

241 2011 (3) SA 347 (CC), at par 179.

242 Section 232 of the constitution reads: "Customary international law is law in the republic unless it is inconsistent with the constitution or an Act of parliament."

243 Judge in the Cape Provincial Division.

244 1971(1) SA 234 (C).

part of their own law. In my view it is the duty of this court to ascertain and administer the appropriate rule of international law.[245]

In *Nduli v Minister of Justice*[246] the court described this rule as an aspect found within Roman Dutch law. Dugard also suggests that the Roman law jurists failed to draw a distinction between international law and municipal law, resulting in Roman Dutch law's following the monist approach.[247] However, there is a limit to the direct applicability of customary international law: where customary international law is inconsistent with the constitution or an act of parliament, it is invalid.[248] This is a rare feature of the direct application principle. Elsewhere in such systems in normal circumstances no limit is placed on the direct applicability of customary international law Direct applicability is intertwined with the supremacy of the international provisions, and subjecting customary international law to the constitution and legislative acts clouds the direct applicability of customary international law, thus implying that this is not monism in its true sense.

The concept of a self-executing international agreement is a product of the monist theory.[249] An international agreement that is considered to be a self-executing agreement is an agreement that will be directly applicable. Section 231(4) of the constitution provides:

> ...but a self-executing provision of an agreement that has been approved by parliament is law in the Republic unless it is inconsistent with the Constitution or an Act of Parliament.[250]

The principle of self-executing international agreements is borrowed from the United States, where it has caused much controversy.[251] However, the USA courts have ruled in instances where an agreement is of reciprocal duty that such an agreement is self-executing. The United States court of customs and patents appeals hearing the matter

---

245 1971(1) SA 234 (C).
246 1978 (1) SA 893 (A). "The *fons et origo* of this proposition must be found in Roman Dutch law"
247 Dugard Commenting on *Nduli v Minister of Justice*: "This served as an important reminder that the rule favouring the incorporation of customary international law into South African law is derived from Roman-Dutch law and not English law".
248 Dugard *EJIL* 1997"As a species of common law, customary international law is, however, subordinate to all forms of legislation".77
249 Ngolele *SAYIL* 2006 31 170.
250 Section 231(4).
251 Dugard *International law: A South African Perspective* 56.

John T Bill Co., Inc. Victor Distributing Co. v United States [252]ruled to that effect.[253] Considering most REI agreements are of a reciprocal nature, this could be helpful to REI agreements in South Africa, with the exception of the limitation clause that follows self-execution agreements.

The South African courts themselves have never been able to give a definitive response to what amounts to a self-executing treaty. In the matter between *President of the Republic of South Africa v Quagliani*[254]Sachs CJ in his judgement was sceptical in his consideration of whether the bilateral agreement between South Africa and the USA was a self-executing treaty or not. He gave the impression that international agreements were all the same in the long run, and the procedure according to which they came to have the effect of law was not important. He expressed the following opinion:[255]

> The question then is whether the agreement becomes law in South Africa as contemplated by section 231(4) of the constitution. There are two ways in which this question can be answered. The first is to say that the agreement itself does not become binding in domestic law, but the international obligation the agreement encapsulates is given effect to by the provisions of the Act. The second approach is that once the agreement has been entered into as specified in section 2 and 3 of the Act, it becomes law in South Africa as contemplated by section 231 (4) of the constitution without further legislation by parliament. [47] It is not necessary for the purposes of this case to decide which of these approaches is correct, for their effect in this case is the same.

The effect may well be the same but the process by which enactment takes place is totally different. This was the main issue that the Constitutional Court (hereinafter referred to as CC) had to decide by highlighting what amounts to a self-executing agreement and how it was different from any general international agreement. Sachs J's finding in this instance is rather evasive and avoids the real challenges embroiled within section 231(4). Ferreira and Scholtz lament:[256]

> It must right at the outset be emphasised that in avoiding the question whether the extradition agreement could be viewed as self – executing, the constitutional court

252 Published in *AMJIL* Vol 35 No 1 pp 160-169, May 29 1939.

253 The treaty was reciprocal and it was self-executing, requiring no legislation other than its own enactment, so far as any matter here involved was concerned.

254 [2009] ZACC 1.

255 [2009] ZACC 1.

256 Ferreira and Scholtz *CILSA* 2009,269.

missed a golden opportunity to determine the content of one of the most controversial issues in section 231 of the constitution.

The failure of the constitutional court to define what amounts to a self-executing agreement could have been remedied by the judiciary when it interpreted the law. However, the highest court of the land, the CC, was evasive in determining what amounts to a self-executing agreement, thus providing a loophole for the entry of uncertainty. On the other hand, it is possible that Sachs CJ in his judgement was hinting at the possibility that the bilateral extradition agreement between South Africa and USA was self-executing when he stated it did not need parliamentary ratification for it to have the force and effect of law.[257]He stated:[258]

> I conclude therefore, that on either of the approaches identified above, no further enactment by parliament is required to make extradition between South Africa and the United States permissible in South African law.

Perhaps South Africa's challenge emanates from the fact that the constitution itself does not define what constitutes a self-executing agreement. Botha has rightly found the following:[259]

> First the constitution, although introducing the concept of self-execution, fails to define it. Therefore, whenever the question of whether or not a specific treaty is self-executing arises, the court will need to define what self-execution means. The classic (and largely meaningless) definition generally cited in both the *Qugliani* and *Goodwin Cases* in the courts *a quo* is that a self-executing treaty is one which operates of itself without the need for any further legislative provision.

The second challenge that South Africa faces is that, after having introduced the principle of direct applicability relating to international agreements, those same agreements have to be measured up against the constitutional and parliamentary processes. This again clouds the direct applicability of such agreements as they are subjected to the municipal laws of South Africa. Subscribing to monism with traces of dualism as in the discussion of self-executing international agreements negates the need for making some provisions

---

257 Ferreira and Scholtz XLII *CILSA* 2009.
258 [2009] ZACC 1 par 48.
259 Botha 2009 *SAYIL* 266.

self-executing in the first instance and makes the whole idea of self-execution meaningless within South African constitutional provisions.

Self-executing agreements will be valid only as long as they fall in line with constitutional provisions and acts of parliament. Ngolele seems to have affirmed this constitutional position without giving consideration to the true nature of direct applicability. He states:[260]

> Direct applicability does not necessarily imply that the treaty or customary international law in question has legal force within municipal law. That is, automatic or direct applicability does not necessarily confer validity upon customary international law. Validity depends on consistency with the constitution and Acts of parliament. Consequently, a treaty might be directly applicable within municipal law but found to be invalid.

Direct applicability within the South African context has been intertwined with the supremacy of its laws, which distorts its true meaning. Direct applicability in its true sense would mean the international agreements would reign supreme over municipal laws, and their validity would not be measured against the municipal laws of a state.[261] Ngolele's pronouncement complicates the true meaning of direct applicability and goes to show the complexities that are bound to surface when a dualist country tries to implement monist principles such as self–execution in what is dominantly dualist legal setting.

Presupposing that an REI agreement entered into by South Africa is self-executing, the constitution provides that such an agreement is valid only if it has been approved by parliament and is in accordance with the constitution and acts of parliament. Such an approach will delay the process of realising REI.

4.2.2 The Dualist theory and international agreements within South Africa's constitution

Section 231[262] of the constitution relates to international agreements and how they are received within South Africa's municipal law for them to be binding and have the force of law within the municipal legal system. Section 231 provides a three-tier process which

---

260 Ngolele *SAYIL* 2006 167.

261 See para 3.2.1.

262 Section 231 is devoted to address International agreements.

international agreements have to go through for them to be considered as law within the republic. This three-tier process would apply to any REI agreements South Africa entered into.

Firstly, it is the prerogative of the executive to enter into international agreements.[263] This is the international ratification of the treaty where a deposit of ratification takes place.[264]Sachs J in the case of *President of the Republic of South Africa v Quagliani*[265] stated that this requirement does not require the president alone to enter into international agreements. He stated:

> As mentioned above, section 231(1) and 85(2) of the 1996 constitution removed the treaty making power from the exclusive domain of the president and placed it expressly within the responsibility of the national executive authority functioning as a collective unit. [25] Given the provisions of section 231 of the constitution it is not improper for the president, once the decision to enter into the treaty has been made by the president, to confer other formal aspects relating to the accession to the treaty on other members of the national executive.[266]

The respondents argued that by virtue of the fact that the president did not participate in negotiating the treaty the extradition agreement between South Africa and the USA was invalid. Sachs CJ in his judgement was able to take cognisance of why it was not the exclusive duty of the president alone to enter into international agreements. Botha goes further to address this issue and states:[267]

> One can but agree and in the light of some points to be raised on other aspects of the judgement below, commend the court on its thorough analysis of the presidential power in this context. Personally I would have been sorely tempted to opt for the easy approach. The extradition act is ordinary legislation, the constitution is the supreme law of the land, the extradition act says the president must conclude extradition treaties, the constitution says the national executive concludes all treaties; the supreme law trumps the ordinary legislation.

---

263 Section 231(1) states that "The negotiating and signing of all international agreements is the responsibility of the national executive."

264 2004 29 *SAYIL* 14.

265 2009 (4) BCLR (CC).

266 2009 (4) BCLR (CC) at para 24-25.

267 Botha *SAYIL* 2009 34,258.

Botha suggests that the easy route would be to consider what the supreme law of the land says pertaining to the president's powers in this regard.[268] Section 85(2) of the constitution provides:[269]

> The president exercises the executive authority, together with the other members of the cabinet, by (a) implementing national legislation except where the constitution or an Act of Parliament provides otherwise; (b) developing and implementing national policy; (c) co-ordinating the functions of state departments and administrations;(d) preparing and initiating legislation; and (e) performing any other executive function provided for in the constitution or in national legislation.

The executive's powers do not pertain to the president's personal capacity alone. Other members of the national executive may also enter into agreements. This is evident in the wording of section 231(1) and also in the provisions made under section 85(2) of the constitution.

Secondly, South Africa will be bound at an international level only when a resolution has been passed by the National Assembly and the National Council of Provinces,[270] which process has been dubbed as constitutional ratification.[271] Dugard states: "Section 231(2) is intended to establish that an international agreement binds South Africa on the international level only after it has been approved by both houses of Parliament."[272]

This approach is similar to that described in the *Ponsonby rule,* which prevails in Britain.[273]The *Ponsonby rule* is a notification to the parliament with a short memorandum where the parliament is notified of the crown's intention to enter into an international agreement. Such an agreement binds Britain on the international level and has no force or effect in Britain's municipal laws.[274]

---

268 Section 2 of the Constitution reads: "This constitution is the supreme law of the Republic; law or conduct inconsistent with it is invalid, and the obligations imposed by it must be fulfilled."

269 Section 85(2), Constitution of the Republic of South Africa 1996.

270 Section 231(2).

271 The arguments forwarded by Olivier in relation to section 231(2) have been disputed by Dugard, who has clearly brought section 231(2) into context. Dugard states: Section 231(2) is intended to establish that an international agreement binds South Africa on the international level only after it has been approved by both houses of Parliament. To apply domestically a treaty must still be enacted into law by national legislation, as specified in s 231(4).

272 Dugard *International law: A South African Perspective*, 57.

273 Sloss *et al* The role of Domestic Courts in Treaty Enforcement 476-503.

274 Sloss *et al* The role of Domestic Courts in Treaty Enforcement 476.

Lastly, for an international agreement to have the force and effect of law within the municipal laws of South Africa, it must still be enacted into law by national legislation, as specified in s 231(4). This was always the position, even before the adoption of the new constitution. In *Pan-American World Airways Incorporated v SA Fire and Accident Insurance,* the judge provided:[275]

> It is common cause, and trite law I think, that in this country the conclusion of a treaty, convention, or agreement by the South African Government with any other government is an executive and not a legislative act. As a general rule, the provisions of an international instrument so concluded are not embodied in our municipal law except by legislative process. As a general rule, the provisions of an international instrument so concluded are not embodied in our municipal law except by legislative process. The universal Postal Convention and the bilateral Air Transport agreement are no exceptions. In the absence of any enactment giving their relevant provisions the force of law, they cannot affect the rights of the subject.

Ngcobo CJ in the minority judgement of the *Glenister Case* reiterated:

> It is implicit, if not explicit, from the scheme of section 231, that an international agreement that becomes law in our country enjoys the same status as any other legislation. This is so because it is enacted into law by national legislation, and can only be elevated to a status superior to that of other national legislation if parliament expressly indicates its intent that the enacting legislation should have such status.[276]

Parliamentary ratification is the only means that has been accepted for international agreements to have the force or effect of law within the South African legal system. For the purposes of REI, the need for parliamentary ratification would slow down the realisation of REI. Dugard states:[277]

> This took no account of the fact that many treaties are intended to come into operation immediately, and that slow parliamentary ratification would undermine the value of such treaties.

Parliamentary ratification is deemed as a sovereign act that an independent state such as South Africa can exercise. Ngcobo CJ in the *Glenister case* stated: [278]

---

275 1965(3) SA 150 (A).

276 Minority judgement in the *Glenister Case* par 100.

277 Dugard *International law: A South African perspective* 54.

278 2011 (3) SA 347 (CC), at para 91.

> The approval of an international agreement under section 231(2) of the constitution conveys South Africa's intention, in its capacity as a sovereign state, to be bound at an international level by the provisions of the agreement.

Although South Africa is a sovereign state, it must understand that when it steps into the arena of community law, its sovereignty is not absolute. South Africa cannot rely on its sovereignty as a means to evade its obligations at an international level. As Pescatore avers, "...the preconceived idea of indivisible sovereignty blinds men's minds to the phenomenon of integration."[279] The issue of sovereignty thwarts the powers of the SADC to the extent that it cannot exercise its powers within SA's legal domain simply because South Africa will uphold its sovereignty. This negatively affects the implementation of SADC laws and prevents the realisation of REI.[280]

Moseneke DCJ and Cameron DCJ at para 193 stated with reference to South Africa's obligation stemming from international agreements:[281]

> That is a duty this country itself undertook when it acceded to these international agreements, and it is an obligation that became binding on the Republic, in the international sphere, when the National assembly and the National Council of Provinces by resolution adopted them, more especially the U.N Convention.

This approach clearly identifies with the monist approach, where the laws directly apply without the need for parliamentary ratification. Cameron pronounced further:[282]

> It follows that the constitution places an obligation on lawmakers to pay heed to the republic's international obligations when drafting legislation. While section 231 does not have the effect of elevating all international obligations to the status of constitutional obligations, it does mean (when read with other provisions of the constitution) that the state's international obligations are enforceable to some degree on the domestic plane, by domestic actors.

The judiciary acknowledged that where human rights are concerned, international obligations ratified on an international plane give rise to enforceable rights in the municipal plane to those affected by such agreements. This is in accordance with section

---

279 Pescatore *Law of integration* 32.
280 Saurombe Common problems affecting supranational attempts.
281 Moseneke and Cameron Glenister Case.
282 Cameron *Duke J of CIL* vol 23. 406.

39(1) (c), which provides that when interpreting the bill of rights courts must consider international law. Ferreira and Snyman applaud the constitutional court in this regard, stating:[283]

> It must be emphasised that the majority judgement's approach, although limited to bill of rights issues, is to be welcomed as it is fairly in line with the constitutional court's earlier findings that the bill of rights must be interpreted extensively, which is to suggest that it should relate not only to the contents of the individual rights but also to any unnecessary stumbling blocks in the way of realising the particular rights.

This is a positive move and hopefully the same approach will be taken for REI agreements where constitutional ratification will be more than enough for REI agreements to have the force and effect of law within South Africa's municipal laws without their having to be enacted as legislation to be valid.

4.3 The dualist approach on REI agreements: loophole for unilateral revocation of REI agreements? A SCA perspective

Reducing international agreements to acts of parliament and affording REI agreements the same status as acts of parliament weakens the REI agenda, because within the hierarchy of laws the *lex posterior, derogate priori* rule will apply. The rule implies that subsequent acts of parliament can render ineffective a community law that has been incorporated into municipal law by a prior act.[284]Oppong observes:[285]

> In economic integration, the application of this rule to community law upsets the vertical relations between community and national legal systems, hinders the uniform application of community law within the member states legal systems and generally makes community law ineffective.

Such an approach could result in the unilateral revocation of REI agreements, whereby a member state introduces new acts of parliament that repeal an act which carries with it an international obligation which ought to be upheld. This would leave room for inconsistencies within the REC as some member states would still be upholding REI

---

283 Ferreira and Snyman *PELJ* 2014 17(4)1482.

284 Oppong *Legal aspects of economic integration* 191.

285 Oppong *Making regional economic communities enforceable* 3.

agreements whilst in other member states' municipal laws the agreement would have been repealed by an act of parliament.

Such an effect was evident in the supreme court of appeal (SCA) decision on *A Moola Group v Commissioner for SARS.*[286] This case was primarily centred on the trade bilateral agreement entered into by South Africa's national executive with the government of the Republic of Malawi.[287] Section 49 of the *Customs and Excise Act*[288]requires such an agreement (pertaining to the lowering of customs duty and granting preferential treatment) to be enacted as law after being published as a notice in the government gazette.[289] Article 2 of the bilateral agreement reads:

> Subject to the provisions of this agreement the Government of the Republic of South Africa shall allow all goods grown, produced or manufactured in Malawi, to be imported into South Africa free of customs duty.[290]

What amounted to goods produced or manufactured in Malawi was expounded by article 6 (ii), which reads:

> Goods shall not be regarded as having been produced or manufactured:
> (iii) in Malawi unless at least 25 percent, or such other lower percentage as may from time to time be agreed upon between the parties in respect of specified goods manufactured in Malawi, of the production cost of those goods shall be represented by materials produced and labour performed in Malawi and the last process in the production or manufacture of such goods shall have taken place in Malawi.[291]

The appellant had been importing garments manufactured in Malawi free of customs duty for years. The respondent unilaterally decided to revoke the freedom from customs duty provided in this agreement and ordered the appellants to pay customs duty for the latest

---

286 [2003] ZASCA 18.

287 http://www.sars.gov.za.The agreement was entered into in 1990.Section 51 of the Customs and Excise Act provides for the national executive to enter into trade agreements with other countries within the African territories.

288 91 of 1964.

289 Gen Not R1357 in GG 12546 OF 20 June 1990; Section 49 0f the Customs and Excise Act; Dugard *International law: A South African Perspective* states "Three principal methods are employed by the legislature to transform treaties into municipal law. In the first instance, the provisions of a treaty may be embodied in the text of an act of Parliament, secondly, the treaty may be included as a schedule to a statute, and thirdly an enabling Act of Parliament may give the executive the power to bring a treaty into effect in municipal law by means of proclamation or notice in the Government Gazette." 55.

290 Gen Not R1357 in GG 12546 OF 20 June 1990.

291 Gen Not R1357 in GG 12546 OF 20 June 1990.

consignment of garments they imported from Malawi, which was a violation of the South Africa - Malawi trade agreement. Erasmus succinctly puts the respondent's position into perspective when he stated:[292]

> What had to be decided was the interpretation to be given to the concept of production cost. The appellants argued that the imported garments were produced or manufactured in Malawi since 25% of their production cost was represented by materials produced and labour performed in Malawi. The respondents on the other hand, were of the opinion that production cost must be given a meaning by having regard to the provisions of the customs and excise act and the rules made under it.

The respondent wanted the meaning of "production cost" provided in the Customs and Excise Act and rule 46[293] of it to be the determining factor in deciding if the garments had been manufactured in Malawi and were hence free of customs duty. This meant that the meaning of "production cost" as contemplated in the South Africa – Malawi trade agreement would not suffice, as the provisions of the Customs and Excise Act would be adhered to. The respondent averred that the agreement owed its existence to the act, formed part of the act, and was to be construed as such. The SCA seemed to lean to the respondent's arguments, and Lewis AJ stated:

> The agreement is part of the statute. If the provisions in the statute, or the rules made under it, are changed from time to time, so too must the articles of the agreement be interpreted accordingly. No express permission to this effect is required. This conclusion is a logical consequence of the principle discussed earlier that the agreement takes its meaning from the statute of which it forms a part.[294]

The SCA's finding in this regard is rather disturbing, because the meaning that ought to have been given due cognisance to is that of the agreement and not the act. The constitution has also provided that when interpreting the law every court must prefer a reasonable interpretation that is consistent with international law.[295]If REI-related agreements are subjected to acts of parliament and given a subservient status within the

---

292 Erasmus *SAYIL* 2003 161.
293 Calculation for the production cost.
294 Para 21.
295 Section 233 of the constitution reads: "When interpreting any legislation, every court must prefer any reasonable interpretation of the legislation that is consistent with international law over any alternative interpretation that is inconsistent with international law."

municipal laws of South Africa they will fail. The laws of the Republic will be able to disband RECs.

The commissioner's decision to amend an international agreement leaves a lot to be desired. Firstly, in carrying out his administrative action he trumped the legitimate expectation which the appellants had in this instance.[296] There was a well-established practice that the appellants would trade with their Malawian counterparts free of customs duty, and unilaterally taking that privilege away thwarted the appellants' expectation. This view was confirmed in Australia in the *Teoh Case,*[297]where it was determined that entering into an international agreement can give rise to a legitimate expectation. In this case Toohey J held that: [298]

> ...the assumption of such an obligation may give rise to legitimate expectation in the minds of those who are affected by administrative decisions on which the obligation has some bearing.

It is of importance to state that trade agreements require certainty to ensure that effective trade takes place and that ultimately REI will be achieved. Erasmus states:[299]:

> States do not trade, private businesses do. International trade transactions take place in terms of contractual arrangements between importers and exporters. But the movement of goods, services and capital across state boundaries inevitably involves interstate regulation.

With that in mind, administrators must not distort the trading plane by unilaterally altering trade agreements at the expense of citizens and disregarding the state's obligations at international level. Secondly, the commissioner's powers in this regard were a thorough deviation from section 231(2) of the constitution. Erasmus, commenting on A J Lewis' averments,[300] states:[301]

> This is a somewhat startling observation. It in fact means that domestic authorities can from time to time, in terms of their discretionary powers, change the meaning and content of international agreements. What gives rise to even greater concern, is

---

296 See Chapter 3.
297 See Chapter 3.3.2 Enforcing the Campbell decision and public policy.
298 Australian supreme court.
299 Erasmus *SAYIL* 28(1) 164.
300 Lewis AJ judgement para 21.
301 Erasmus SAYIL 28(1) 180.

the fact that this statement also applies to those agreements concluded in terms of section 231(2) of the constitution and falling into the category approved by parliament. Officials would then be free to alter parliament's decisions on how and to what extent international obligations bind the republic. They can change the meaning and effect of treaty obligations.

There is a legislative presumption that in enacting the law the legislature did not intend to violate its international obligations.[302] In *Azanian People's Org v President of the Republic of South Africa*[303] the court expressed the opinion that: "The lawmakers of the constitution should not lightly be presumed to authorise any law which might constitute a breach of the obligations of the State in terms of international law."[304]

Six years after the *A Moola* decision[305] it seems that the SCA has taken a divergent view in similar matters. In *Progress Office Machine v SARS*[306]the appellant was an importer of paper which he sold on the domestic market. In this particular case the appellant imported paper from Indonesia which came to him via the Durban port, and paid his customs duty accordingly. The appellant thereafter received a letter from the first respondent,[307] informing him that an investigation had been carried out and he was liable to pay anti–dumping duty to the amount of one million five hundred and sixty-five thousand, five hundred and sixty-nine dollars and sixty cents (R 1 565 569-60).

The appellant contended that the first respondent's decision was against international law emanating from the *Uruguay Round,*[308] which revamped the General Agreement on Tariffs and Trade (GATT)[309]and led to the formation of the World Trade Organisation under the *Marrakesh Agreement,*[310]of which South Africa was one of the founding members.

---

302 Dugard "The place of international law in South African Municipal law" 64.
303 1996 (4) SA 671.
304 1996 (4) SA 671 para 26.
305 [2003] ZASCA 18.
306 2008 (2) SA 13 (SCA).
307 SARS.
308 The 8th round of multilateral trade negotiations.
309 GATT 1994 following the *Uruguay round.*
310 Agreement Establishing the World Trade Organisation 1 January 1995.

During the *Uruguay Round* member states agreed under article 11.3 that anti-dumping duties would be imposed for a period not exceeding five years.[311] It was the appellant's case that the five-year period had elapsed, considering that the five-year period had started on the 27th of November 1998 and ended on the 27th of November 2003,[312]whereas the respondent argued that the five-year period started when the Minister of Finance, acting under section 55(2) of the Customs and Excise act, made the publication in the Government Gazette.[313]

However, the imposition made by the Minister of Finance in exercising his administrative powers was limitless and did not stipulate when the anti–dumping duties would cease to apply. Malan AJA in this instance ruled:[314]

> Not only is a court bound to prefer any reasonable interpretation of the legislation that is consistent with international law, but subordinate legislation such as the notice by the Minister of Finance imposing the anti-dumping duty must be reasonable. The duration of the anti-dumping duty imposed beyond the period allowed by the anti-dumping agreement would not only be a breach of the republic's international obligations and an unreasonable interpretation of the notice but also unreasonable and to that extent invalid.

This line of reasoning is consistent with section 233 of the Constitution, which reads:

> When interpreting any legislation, every court must prefer any reasonable interpretation of the legislation that is consistent with international law over any alternative interpretation that is inconsistent with international law.

The approach of making sure that the laws are made to be consistent with international agreements taken by Malan AJ is much appreciated and would be helpful for the purposes

311 Article 11.3 reads "Notwithstanding the provisions of paragraphs 1 and 2, any definitive anti-dumping duty shall be terminated on a date not later than five years from its imposition(or from the date of the most recent review under paragraph 2 if that review has covered both dumping and injury or under this paragraph),unless the authorities determine, in a review initiated before the date on their own initiative or upon a duly substituted request made by or on or behalf of the domestic industry within a reasonable period of time prior to that date, that the expiry of the duty would be likely to lead to continuation or recurrence of dumping and injury."

312 Malan AJ para 12.

313 Malan AJA para 11:"The act gives powers to the Minister of Finance to amend schedule 2 to impose anti-dumping duty in accordance with section 55(2) and to withdraw or reduce any anti-dumping duty imposed by him. In exercising powers under section 55(2), the Minister of Finance imposed anti-dumping duty by GN R 685GG 20125 of 28 May 1999 without stipulating the period of time the duty would be operative." 8.

314 Malan AJA para 11.

of attaining REI. It lays the basis for certainty within REI agreements, thus making REI attainable.

4.3.1 The Constitutional Court's approach to REI agreements

As mentioned earlier, the *Glenister* decision was delivered in one of the landmark cases where the Constitutional Court of South Africa had to address the status of international agreements in South Africa. In *Glenister* the applicant took the South African government to task for not establishing an independent anti–corruption unit which would effectively function without due influence from other spheres of the government sector.

It was the applicant's argument, supported by the Helen Suzman Foundation[315] which was amicus curiae,[316] that South Africa had an international obligation to ensure an independent anti-corruption unit was established. The international agreements that the *amicus curiae* referred to were the *United Nations Convention against Corruption*[317] and the *Prevention and Combating of Corrupt Activities Act*.[318]

In delivering the majority judgement, Moseneke DCJ and Cameron DCJ stressed South Africa's obligations at a continental level and within the SADC. Reference was made to the SADC *Protocol on Combating Illicit Drug Trafficking,*[319] which provided under Article 8[320] the need to establish an independent anti-corruption unit.

---

315 The Foundation promotes liberal constitutional democracy. Helen Suzman Foundation 2013 http://www.hsf.org.za.

316 This is a Latin term which when translated refers to a friend of the court. Such a "friend" is not party to an action but petitions the court or is invited by the court to provide information or submit its views because it has a strong interest in the case. Mubangizi *Constructing the* Amicus Curiae *procedure in Human Rights Litigation* 2012 *LDD* 199.

317 United Nations Convention against Corruption (2005).

318 12 of 2004.

319 Protocol on Combating Illicit Drug Trafficking 1996.

320 A 8 provides that: (1) Member states shall institute appropriate and effective measures for co-operation between enforcement to curb corruption resulting from illicit drug trafficking.(2) Measures to be taken shall include the following:

(a) establishment of adequately resourced anti-corruption agencies or units that are:-

(i) Independent from undue intervention through appointment and recruiting mechanisms that generate the designation of persons of high professional quality and integrity.

(ii) Free to initiate and conduct investigations;

(iii) Capable of gathering evidence, examining files and documents, and having the power to administer oaths and to deal with any obstruction and contempt.

The Constitutional Court took cognisance of the need to curb corruption as a means to realise sustainable development and economic growth within the SADC, which is what the REI agenda seeks to achieve. Moseneke DCJ and Cameron DCJ stated:[321]

> When corruption and organised crime flourish, sustainable development and economic growth are stunted. And in turn, the stability and security of society is put at risk. [167] This deleterious impact of corruption on societies and the pressing need to combat it concretely and effectively is widely recognised in public discourse, in our legislation, in regional and international conventions and academic research.

One of the ills of society, such as corruption in this instance, was duly recognised by South Africa's Constitutional Court as an obstacle to growth and development, which are the intended objectives of REI in the SADC.

Recently the constitutional court delivered a judgment that promoted the REI in the SADC in the matter between the *Government of the Republic of Zimbabwe v Fick* [322](*Fick* decision). The constitutional court was hearing a matter on appeal from the North Gauteng High Court (hereinafter referred to as NGHC) and the SCA. The issue in this case concerned the enforcement of an order of costs which had been issued by the SADC tribunal on the government of Zimbabwe, concerning the *Mike Campbell* decision.

In the SCA, Tuchten AJ ordered for the properties of the government of Zimbabwe situated in Cape Town to be attached so as to satisfy the cost order made by the SADC tribunal. When the matter reached the CC, Mogoeng CJ dismissed the appeal and explained South Africa's obligation under the SADC community laws, in particular article 32 of the *SADC Protocol on the SADC Tribunal.*[323]Mogoeng CJ stated:[324]

> Article 32 imposes a duty upon member states, including South Africa, to take all execution-facilitating measures, such as the development of the common law principles on the enforcement of foreign judgements, to ensure execution of decisions of the tribunal. It also gives binding force to the decisions of the tribunal on the parties, including the affected member states, paves the way and provides for the enforceability of the Tribunal's decisions within the territories of member states. South Africa has essentially bound itself to do whatever is legally permissible to deal with

321 2011 (3) SA 347 (CC). para 166-167.
322 2013 (5) SA 325 (CC).
323 Protocol on Tribunal 2005.
324 Mogoeng CJ para 59.

> any attempt by any member state to undermine and subvert the authority of the Tribunal and its decisions as well as the obligations under the amended treaty.

Mogoeng CJ further reiterated that South Africa's obligations did not stem only from the SADC *Protocol on the SADC Tribunal* but also emanated from South Africa's constitutional provisions. He stated:[325]

> Added to this, are our own constitutional obligations to honour our international agreements and give practical expressions to them, particularly when the rights provided for in these agreements, such as the Amended treaty, similar to those provided for in our Bill of Rights, are sought to be vindicated. We are also enjoined by our constitution to develop the common law in line with the spirit, purport and objects of the Bill of Rights.

The enforceable right to which Mogoeng CJ referred was the right of access to courts.[326] He submitted that access to justice does not mean only securing access and being heard in a court of law, but that another component is ensuring that the order given is complied with. In this regard Mogoeng CJ noted: "An observance of the right to access to courts would therefore be hollow if the court order were not to be enforced".[327]

The *Fick* decision goes to show that the South African judiciary recognises South Africa's obligations at a regional level and makes judgements that ensure that SADC community laws are upheld and enforceable. De Wet has applauded the CC for taking a bold step in ensuring that foreign judgements are enforceable within South Africa's municipal order.[328] This creates a sense of certainty, which is shown by the fact that the jurisdictional findings made by the SADC tribunal has been confirmed by all courts of South Africa in their respective divisions.[329] This is key to REI, and the judiciary in this regard has affirmed the importance of REI in the SADC.

---

325 Mogoeng CJ

326 Section 37.

327 Mogoeng CJ at para 62.

328 De Wet 2014 *PER* "It was the first time since its inception that the constitutional court was confronted with the status of a binding international decision within the domestic legal order." 554.

329 *Government of the Republic of Zimbabwe v Fick and Others* [2012] ZASCA 122; *Louis Karel Fick v Government of the Republic of Zimbabwe* unreported case number 3106/07 of January 2010.

4.4 Conclusion

This chapter has sought to give a detailed analysis of South Africa's approach to legal reception and how its approach impacts upon the realisation of REI at municipal level. It is now clear that the hybrid theory that applies to South Africa's constitution has somehow clouded the manner in which South Africa adopts international agreements. The way in which the monist theory is applied shows that it distorts its true meaning, as it has traces of the dualist theory accompanying it. This complicates the use of the law as a strategy to effect REI.

It has also been demonstrated that the South African judiciary has passed judgements that ensure certainty and affirm the objectives and purpose which the SADC seeks to uphold. South Africa's judiciary is to be applauded for its gradual application and interpretation of SADC laws, as this has the potential to make the implementation of the laws a feasible strategy in the realisation of REI as envisaged by the RISDP of the SADC. However, as one of the economically strong powers within the region, there is a need for South Africa to continue to uphold the rule of law so as not to threaten the efficacy of REI at a regional level.

Chapter 5: Conclusion and recommendations

At the heart of REI in Southern Africa lies the need to uplift the people of the region economically and to attain the post-2015 SDG.[330] From a legal perspective, a contributory factor that is hampering the completion of REI and therefore the achievement of the above goals is the vagaries of legal reception in the region.[331] The aim of this research paper was to determine how the different approaches to legal reception prescribed by the two Southern African RECs impact upon the realisation of REI.[332]

In order to answer the above research question, Chapter 2 introduced the phenomenon of REI and how it fits into the legal context. The chapter established that although REI is governed by international law (since it relates to interstate relations), it falls under a special kind of international law, which is community law.[333] Furthermore, and through the legal prism, the chapter tested the proposition of legal integration as a means to realising REI. In this regard, legal integration was defined to mean the uniform application of REI to create legal certainty, which is essential for the completion of REI processes.[334] However, the legal obstacle that prevents legal integration is legal reception. The different approaches to legal reception- the monist theory, the dualist theory and the hybrid theory - were then discussed.[335] To demonstrate how these different approaches and the challenges they present influence REI, the study evaluated legal reception within the EEC context.

It was established that sixty-three percent of member states in the EEC followed a dualist approach when it came to the incorporation of international law within their municipal laws. Despite the fact that dualism stands in the way of realising REI, the EEC was able to ensure the uniform application of its laws through three decisions relating to legal integration. Most importantly, the judicial arm was the driving force which gave decisions

330 See para 1.1.
331 See para 1.2.
332 See para 1.2.
333 See para 2.2.1.
334 See para 2.2.1.
335 See para 2.3.

that ensured the direct applicability of EEC laws in member states' municipal laws.[336]The supremacy of the EEC laws led to the attainment of REI in the EEC,[337] and the member states were compelled to surrender a part of their sovereignty.[338]

Chapter 3 established the framework within which REI has been conceptualised and approached in Africa. On a continental level, the legal framework to REI was traced from the *Abuja Treaty* to the *AU Constitutive Act,*[339]as was its becoming a mandate for action on the sub-regional level.[340] On a regional level, the study focused on the experiences of Southern Africa and its existing RECs, namely the SADC and the COMESA. Both of these RECs have recognised that law can be used as a means to complete the process of REI. However, the challenge of legal reception also exists within Southern Africa,[341] as the legal frameworks in the two RECs themselves follow the dualist approach to legal reception (as a means to ensuring REI laws have force and effect within the member states municipal laws).

Chapter 3 also found that the SADC and the COMESA have left the incorporation and application of their laws to their member states. Given that sixty percent of the countries in Southern Africa follow a dualist approach to legal reception, leaving the application and incorporation of REC laws to member states (through their constitutional or other legislative provisions), which could be detrimental to REI for a number of reasons. Firstly, this would mean that the laws relating to REI are not supreme over municipal laws, as they could be repealed by an act of parliament.[342]Secondly, member states have a supremacy clause within their constitutional provisions which creates an exit approach for them as a means to evade their obligations within the international community (as exemplified by the experiences of the Zimbabwean and Mauritian governments).[343] Thirdly, as a result of their colonial legacies, most Southern African states embrace sovereignty as a principle, with the result that subjecting the application and incorporation

336 See para 2.4.1.
337 See para 2.4.2.
338 See para 2.4.3.
339 See para 2.6.
340 See para 2.6.1.
341 See para 3.2.
342 See paras 3.2.3, 3.2.6, 3.3.3.
343 See paras 3.2.3 3.3.1.

of REI laws to municipal laws is subjecting these laws to the sovereignty of the member states.[344] Lastly, the process of parliamentary ratification delays the effect of REI laws, as it takes a while for parliamentary ratification to occur, and therefore for an agreement to become enforceable.

Chapter 3 also discussed the role of the REC judiciary. The chapter found that unlike the situation in the EEC where the ECJ plays an active role in the interpretation and determination of EEC LAWS, the SADC tribunal, which serves countries within the SADC block, is currently suspended and dysfunctional.[345] While the COMESA Court of Justice is still fully functional and still has its authority intact,[346] not all member states of the SADC are members of COMESA.

In Chapter 4 the study moved from the general to the particular by analysing legal reception within the South African context. As one of the most economically advanced states in Southern Africa, South Africa has economically benefited and contributed to REI in Southern Africa. The chapter established that South Africa applies the hybrid theory to legal reception, in which a monist approach is followed in relation to customary international law and a dualist approach in relation to international agreements inclusive of REI agreements[347] However, the South African judiciary has made pronouncements on the validity and importance of REC laws for the attainment of REI. Thus, through an analysis of South African cases it has been established that there is a gradual move from South Africa's judiciary to reject a dualist approach to regional law and apply a monist interpretation instead.

Overall, the study has established that the approach to legal reception by the two RECs in Southern Africa impacts negatively on the realisation of REI. What would have been ideal in this instance is a clear legal framework which encompasses the principles of law that ensure that legal reception does not impede the attainment of REI. These principles should include the direct applicability of REI laws in member states' municipal laws, the

---

344 See para 3.2.1.1.
345 See para 3.6.
346 See para 3.6.
347 See paras 4.2 and 4.3.

supremacy of REI laws over municipal laws, the independence of the judiciary, and limited sovereignty. Such principles have been shown to be effective in the metamorphosis of the EEC into the EU. While the EU and Southern Africa are quite different when it comes to levels of development (legal, political and economic), these principles worked for the EEC when it was in its developmental stage. Arguably, they could work for Southern Africa, particularly because it is a region in the process of development. However, because of the demographics of laws and politics in Southern Africa, there is no uniformity in the application of REC laws, the REC judiciary in the SADC has been disbanded, and the states still cling to full territorial sovereignty. Full REI will not be possible when states operate with full sovereignty and when there is no proper functional REC judiciary.

In order to address these problems, it would be appropriate to adopt a top down approach in which the founding treaties of the two RECs provide for legal integration, to ensure that the treaties themselves are the means to attain legal integration and therefore REI. However, the lack of political will in these organisations makes it unlikely that this will become a reality. The members of the organisations are unlikely to be willing to cede authority and sovereignty to a regional body.

Alternatively, at the municipal level, when judges interpret or make decisions related to REI laws they take give cognisance of the supranational nature of the RECs, which was the case with most member states in the EEC that were core dualist member states.[348] This would contribute to creating a uniform approach and interpretation of the law and that be conducive to member states' achieving and fulfilling their obligations at the regional level. Creating a stable legal framework would yield legal and economic certainty, which are key factors in enabling the realisation of the post-2015 SDGs in Southern Africa and in the African continent at large.

---

348 See para 2.4.

BIBLIOGRAPHY

Literature

Ambani "Navigating Past the Dualist Doctrine"

Ambani "Navigating Past the Dualist Doctrine: The case for progressive jurisprudence on the application on international human rights norms in Kenya "in Killander M and Adjoholun H "*International Law and Domestic human rights litigation in Africa: An Introduction*" (PULP Cape Town 2010)

Balassa *The Theory of Economic Integration*

Balassa B "*The theory of Economic Integration*"(George Allen and Unwin Ltd London 1962)

Barnard 2015 CILSA

Barnard M "Legal reception in the AU against the backdrop of the Monist/Dualist dichotomy" 2015 CILSA 144-161

Botha 2009 SAYIL

Botha N "Re-writing the Constitution: The strange alchemy of Justice Sachs: indeed"2009 SAYIL 253-267

Burley and Mattli 1993 IO

Burley A and Mattli W "Europe Before the court: A political theory of legal integration" 1993 IO 41-76

Cameron Duke J of Comp Law

Cameron E "Constitutionalism, Rights and International Law: The Glenister Decision"

Cassese *International Law*

Cassese *International Law* (Oxford University Press New York 2001)

Ciongaru 2012 UGBC

Ciongaru "The monist and the dualist theory in European Law" 2012 UGBC 213-232

De Wet 2013 ICSID review

De Wet E "The Rise and fall of the Tribunal of the Southern African Development Community: Implications for Dispute Settlement in Southern Africa" 2013 ICSID review 1-19

De Wet 2014 PELJ

De Wet E "The case of Government of the Republic of Zimbabwe v Louis Karel Fick: A First step towards developing a doctrine of the Status of International Judgements within the Domestic Legal order" 2014 PELJ 554-565

Dugard *International Law*

Dugard J *International Law: A Southern African Perspective*

Dugard 1997 EJIL

Dugard J "International law and the South African Constitution"1997 *EJIL* 77-92

Elivira and Pinedo *EC and EEA Law*

Elivira M and Pinedo M "*EC and EEA Law: A comparative study of the effectiveness of European Law*" (Europa Law publishing Amsterdam 2009)

Erasmus *The New Protocol for the SADC Tribunal*

Erasmus G "*The New Protocol for the SADC Tribunal: Jurisdictional changes and implications for the SADC Community Law*" (TRALAC Stellenbosch 2015)

Erasmus 2003 SAYIL

Erasmus "The incorporation of trade agreements and rules of origin: The extent of constitutional guidance " 2003 SAYIL 157- 181

Fagbayibo 2013 PER

Fagbayibo B "Common Problems Affecting Supranational Attempts in Africa: An Analytical Overview" 2012 CILSA 64-76

Fagbayibo 2012 CILSA

Fagobayibe B "Exploring Legal imperatives of Regional Integration in Africa" 2012 CILSA 64-76

Fagbayibo 2011 SAYIL

Fagbayibo "Re-thinking the African Integration Process" 2011 SAYIL 209-225

Ferreira-Snyman *The Erosion of Sovereignty in Public International Law*

Ferreira-Snyman MP *The Erosion of Sovereignty in Public International Law: Towards World Law?* (LLD Thesis University of Johannesburg 2009)

Ferreira and Ferreira-Snyman 2014 PELJ

Ferreira G and Ferreira-Snyman A "The Incorporation of Public International Law into Municipal Law and Regional Law against the Background of the Dichotomy between Monism and Dualism" 2014 PELJ 1471-1496

Ferreira and Scholtz 2009 CILSA

Ferreira G and Scholtz W "Has the Constitutional Court found the last ball in the high weeds? The interpretation of section 231 of the South African constitution" 2009 CILSA 264-271

Geldnhuys 2012 AI

Geldnhuys D "The African Union and Sovereignty as a Responsibility" 2012 AI 53-67

Hailu 2014 MizanL.Rev

Hailu M B "Regional Economic Integration in Africa Challenges and Prospects" 2014 Mizan.L.Rev 299-332

Hartley *The Foundations of European Community Law*

Hartley *The Foundations of European Community Law* 5th ed (Oxford University Press New York 2003)

Hatzernburg *Regional Integration in Africa*

Hatzernburg T *Regional Integration in Africa* (WTO Economic Research and Statistics Division Geneva2011)

Hay 1965 UIIIL.F

Hay P "International and supranational organisations some problems of conceptualisation" 1965 UIIIL.F 730-770

Killander and Adjolohoun *International Law and domestic human rights*

Killander M and Adjoloun H *International law and domestic human rights litigation in Africa: An Introduction* (PULP Cape Town 2010)

Keleman and Schmidt 2011 JEPP

Keleman R.D and Schmidt SK "The European Court of Justice and Legal Integration: Perpetual momentum?" 2011 JEPP

Kumm 2004 Va J Int'L

Kumm M "International Law and International Courts: The international Rule of Law and the Limits of the International Model" 2004 Va J Int'L 19-32

Lokule-Sodipe and Osuntogun 2013 PER

Lokule-Sodipe J O and Osuntogun AJ "The Quest for a Supranational Entity in West Africa: Can the Economic Community of West African States attain the Status?"2013 PER 255-291

Malan 2012 De Jure

Malan k "The rule of law versus decisionism in the South African constitutional discourse" 2012 De Jure 272-305

Mancuso 2011 J Comp L

Mancuso S "Creating mixed jurisdictions: Legal integration in the SADC" 2011 J Comp L 146-160

Marquis 1977 Syr J Int L and Com

Marquis H.L "Legal integration in the common market"1977 Syr J Int L and Com 207-234

Ngolele 2006 SAYIL

Ngolele EM "The Content of the Doctrine of self-execution and its limited effect in South African Law" 2006 SAYIL 141-172

Oppong 2007 Fordham Int'L J

Oppong "Re –Imagining international law: An examination of recent trends in the reception of international law into national legal systems in Africa" 2007 Fordham Int'L J 296-345

Oppong *Making REC laws enforceable in national legal systems*

Oppong RF "Making REC laws enforceable in national legal systems" *in Monitoring Regional Integration in Southern Africa* (TRALAC Stellenbosch 2008)149-178

Oppong *Legal* aspect of Economic Integration in Africa

Oppong RF *Legal aspects of Economic Integration in Africa* (Cambridge University Press New York 2011)

Pescatore *Law of Integration*

Pescatore P *The law of integration: emergence of a new phenomenon in international relations based on the experience of the European Communities* (Sijthoff Leiden 1974)

Pescatore *Interpretation of Community Law and the Doctrine of Acte Clair*

Pescatore P "Interpretation of Community Law and the 'Doctrine of *ActeClair*'" in Bathurst M E *et al Legal problems of an enlarged European community* (Stevens and Sons London 1972) 41-45

Pitarakis and Tridmas 2003 EJLE

Pitarakis J and Tridmas G "Dynamics of Legal and Economic Integration in the European Union" 2003 EJLE 357-368

Ruppel and Bangamwabo *The SADC Tribunal*

Ruppel O.C and Bangamwabo F.X "The SADC Tribunal: A legal analysis of its mandate and role of regional integration in Southern Africa" in *Monitoring Regional Integration in Southern Africa* (TRALAC Stellenbosch 2008)

Saurombe 2012 SAPL

Saurombe A "An analysis of economic integration in Africa with specific reference to the African Union and the African Economic Community" 2012 SAPL 292-314

Saurombe 2013 LDD

Saurombe "The European Union as a model for regional integration in the Southern African Development Community: A selective institutional comparative analysis" 2013 LDD 457-475

Simon 2010 SAGJ

Simon "The changing context for regional integration in Southern Africa: How adaptive are its regional institutions?" 2010 SAGJ 96-104

Sloss et al *The Role of Domestic Courts in Treaty Enforcement*

Sloss D et al *The Role of Domestic Courts in Treaty Enforcement: A Comparative Study* (Cambridge University Press New York 2009)

Scholtz and Ferreira 2011 ZaoRV

Scholtz W and Ferreira G "Much Ado about Nothing? The SADC Tribunal's Quest for the Rule of Law pursuant to Regional Integration" 2011 ZaoRV 331-358

Tam "The History of the Court of Justice of the European Union"

Tam D "The History of the Court of Justice of the European Union Since its Origin" in Rosa A *et al The Court of Justice and the Construction of Europe: Analyses and perspectives o sixty years of case law* (Springer Hague 2013) 9-35

Verdross 1949 Am J Int' L

Verdross "On the Concept of International Law" 1949 Am J Int 'L

Vidmar *Norms and Conflicts and Hierarchy in International Law*

Vidmar "Norms and Conflicts and Hierarchy in International Law "in De Wet E and Vidmar J *Hierarchy in International Law: The place of Human Rights* (Oxford University Press Oxford 2011)

Case Law

A Moola Group v Commissioner for SARS [2003] ZASCA 18.

Costa v Enel 15 July 1964

Fics De Henri Ramel v Receveur Des Douanes 81/77

Glenister v The President of the Republic of South Africa 2013(4) 347 CC

Government of the Republic of Zimbabwe v Fick 2013(5) SA 325 (CC)

Gramara Private Ltd v Government of the Republic of Zimbabwe HC333/09 Zimbabwe High Court

Hackl v The Financial Intelligence Unit SCA 10/201

John T Bill Co; Inc. Victor Distributing Co. v United States

McCarthy v Smith [1980] Case 129/79

Mike Campbell Private Ltd v The Republic of Zimbabwe SADC (T) 2/2007

Minister of State for Immigration and Ethnic affairs v A Hin Teoh (1995) 183 CLR

Minister of Economic Affairs v Fromagerie Franco Suisse Le Ski [1972]

National Commissioner of the South African Police Service v Southern African Litigation Centre 2015 (1) SA 315 (CC)

Nduli v Minister of Justice 1978 (1) SA 893 (A)

Pan American World Airways Incorporated v SA Fire and Accident Insurance 1965 (3) SA 150 (A)

Polytol Paints and Adhesive Manufacturers Co. Ltd v The Republic of Mauritius Case No 1 of 2012

President of the Republic of South Africa v Quagliani [2009] ZACC.

Progress Office Machine v SARS 2008(2) SA 13 (SCA)

R v Secretary of State for Transport Ex-Factortame No 7 (2001)

*San Michele v High Authority ECSC.*28 June 1965

South Atlantic Islands Development Corporation Ltd v Buchanan 1971 (1) SA 234 (C)

Southern African Litigation Centre v The Government of the Republic of South Africa Case 277 40/2015

*Tavita v Minister of I*mmigration [1994] NZLR 257

Legislation

Constitution of the Republic of South Africa 1996

European Communities Act 1972 Chapter 68

Proceeds of Criminal Confiscation Act 19 of 2008

Constitution of Zimbabwe Amendment 16 Act of 2000

Constitution of Zimbabwe Amendment 17 Act of 2005

Civil Matters Mutual Assistance Act Chapter 8:02

Customs and Tariff Act 59 of 1969

Prevention and Combating of Corrupt Activities Act 12 of 2004

Implementation of the Rome Statute of the International Criminal Court Act 27 of 2007

International Instruments

Agreement Establishing the World Trade Organisation (1995)

Agreement establishing the Common Market for Eastern and Southern Africa (1994)

Constitutive Act of the African Union (2002)

Egypt –Mauritius bilateral agreement (2003)

General Agreement on Tariffs and Trade (1994)

Monrovia Declaration (1979)

Protocol on Relations between the African Union and the Regional Economic Communities (1998)

Protocol on the Statute of the African Court of Justice and Human Rights (2008)

Rome Statute of the International Criminal Court (1998)

SADC Protocol on combating illicit Drug Trafficking (1996)

SADC Protocol on Tribunal (2005)

South Africa-Malawi Trade Agreement (1990)

Sirte Declaration (1999)

Treaty establishing the Southern African Development Community (1992)

New Protocol on the Tribunal in The Southern African Development Community (2014)

Treaty Establishing the African Economic Community (1991)

Treaty on the Non Proliferation of Nuclear Weapons (1968)

Treaty Establishing the European Coal and Steel Community (1951)

Treaty Establishing the European Economic Community (1957)

United Nations Human Rights Charter (1948)

United Nations Convention against Corruption (1995)

Vienna Convention on the Law of Treaties (1969)

Government Publications

Gen Not R 1357 in GG 12546 OF 20 June 1990.

Internet Sources

African Economic Outlook 2015 http//www.africaneconomicoutlook.org

African Economic Outlook 2015 http://www.africaneconomicoutlook.org accessed 10 August 2015

COMESA date unknown http://about.comesa.int

COMESA date unknown http://about.comesa.int/index.php accessed 10 November 2014

Department of International Relations and Co-operation 2003 http://www.dfa.ac.za

Department of International Relations and Co-operation 2003 http://www.dfa.gov.za/docs/2003/au0815.htm accessed 18 November 2014

Lee 2011 http://www.osisa.org

Lee R 2011 http://www.osisa.org/economic-justice/south-africa-and-regional-economic-integration accessed 29 August 2015

Mckinsey& Company 2010 http://www.Mckinsey.com

Mckinsey& Company 2010 http:www.Mckinsey.co.insights/Africa accessed 19 October 2015

Moghadam 2014 http://www.imf.org

Moghadam R 2014 *Benefits of the Integration in Europe* http://www.imf.org accessed 01/11/2015

Nollkaemper 2008-2015 http://www.worldjusticeproject.org

Nollkaemper A 2008-2015 *The nexus Between the National and the International Rule of Law* http://www.worldjusticeproject.org accessed 03/12/2015

SADC 2012 http://www.sadc.int

SADC 2012 http://www.sadc.int.org accessed 18 November 2014

SARS 2015 http://www.sars.gov.za

SARS 2015http//www.sars.gov.za/Legal/International–Treaties-Agreements/Trade-Agreements/Pages/Malawi accessed 25 August 2015

World Bank Ranking 2015 http//www.doingbusiness.org

World Bank 2015 http//www.doingbusiness.org/rankings accessed 13 August 2015